MORAL ISSUES AND MULTINATIONAL CORPORATIONS

Also by Gerard Elfstrom

*ETHICS FOR A SHRINKING WORLD
MILITARY ETHICS   (*with N. Fotion*)

**Also published by Macmillan*

Moral Issues and Multinational Corporations

Gerard Elfstrom
Assistant Professor of Philosophy
Auburn University, Alabama

MACMILLAN

© Gerard Elfstrom 1991

All rights reserved. No reproduction, copy or transmission of this publication may be made without written permission.

No paragraph of this publication may be reproduced, copied or transmitted save with written permission or in accordance with the provisions of the Copyright, Designs and Patents Act 1988, or under the terms of any licence permitting limited copying issued by the Copyright Licensing Agency, 33–4 Alfred Place, London WC1E 7DP.

Any person who does any unauthorised act in relation to this publication may be liable to criminal prosecution and civil claims for damages.

First published 1991

Published by
MACMILLAN ACADEMIC AND PROFESSIONAL LTD
Houndmills, Basingstoke, Hampshire RG21 2XS
and London
Companies and representatives
throughout the world

Edited and typeset by Povey/Edmondson
Okehampton and Rochdale, England

Printed in Hong Kong

British Library Cataloguing in Publication Data
Elfstrom, Gerard
Moral issues and multinational corporations.
1. Business enterprise. Ethical aspects
I. Title
174.4
ISBN 0–333–52690–2

Contents

	Introduction	1
	The Evolution of Multinational Commerce	4
	A Mature Moral Order	7
	Plan of the Chapters	10
1	**Corporate Moral Accountability**	**12**
	Corporate Moral Agency	13
	The Hobbesian Situation	16
	The Obligation to Seek Profits	18
	Corporate Moral Initiative	19
2	**Structure of Response**	**24**
	The Options	24
	Basic and Secondary Wants	27
	The Obligations of Corporations and of People Within Them	30
3	**Corporate Size and Power**	**35**
	The Dangers of Corporate Leviathans	36
	The Benefits of Multinationals	38
	Present Conditions	40
4	**Cultural and Economic Diversity**	**48**
	Cultural and Ideological Differences	48
	Diverse Economic Conditions	51
	Sketch of Possible Responses	54
5	**Corporate Mobility**	**63**
	The Mobility of Products	63
	Evasion of Control	71
	The Mobility of Resources	73
6	**Political Manipulation**	**77**
	The Role of Corporations in Weapons Transfers	79
	The Case of Panama	81
	The Role of Governments	83

7	**South Africa**	**90**
	The Moral Wrong of Apartheid	91
	The Role of Corporations in South Africa	92
	The Case for Corporate Withdrawal from South Africa	94
8	**Conclusion**	**100**
	Current Barriers to Moral Accountability	101
	Prospects for the Near Future	104
	The Mature Moral Order	106

Notes 111

References 133

Index 139

Introduction

Future historians may come to view the economic integration of the globe as the single most important development of the twentieth century, far surpassing the threat of nuclear war, the spread of Marxism or the human disruption of the environment in its broad and continuing influence on human life. None can presently see the final shape of this evolution, and it is probably in its early phases; yet each passing day brings a single world-wide economy closer to hand.

There are currently single global markets for electronic equipment, computers, armaments, aircraft, automobiles and food. Even unlikely areas, such as advertising and publishing, are rapidly becoming global in scope.[1] Corporate leaders are wont to claim that the pressures of competition make it impossible to cultivate only one corner of the world. They find increasingly that they must compete globally or not at all.[2] Along with the globalization of markets, financial institutions and currency regulation are increasingly world encompassing. Marxist nations have also recognized that they must join the larger economic order if they are to hope for increased material well-being, as was powerfully affirmed in Mikhail Gorbachev's striking 'European Home' address presented to the Council of Europe in Strasbourg in July of 1989.[3] His views are underscored by the fate of nations that have sought to opt out of the global economy. The price, as discovered by Albania and the Republic of Myanmar (formerly Burma), is miserable poverty.[4]

The same advances in transportation and communication that allow a global economy, in fact mandate global competition, also foster the creation of enterprises – multinational corporations – able to scatter portions of their corporate organism across the globe.[5] Multinational corporations are at the center of the globalization, homogenization and growing interdependence of the world economy and will continue to nurture this evolution. Over the years, however, their activity has been blanketed by intense controversy. This controversy has been so fervid and so entangled in national aspiration, political intrigue and material greed that partisans have often been unable to agree on the most basic facts describing multinational corporate endeavor.[6] Nonetheless, it is undeniable that the activities of multinational corporations have sometimes resulted in human suffering, death, social upheaval and economic disruption. In addition, their practices have occasionally transgressed minimal standards of decency and fairness in dealing with others, whether competitors, governments or individual human beings. Environmental pollution, unemployment, unsafe labor standards, shoddy and dangerous goods, and the ever-expanding traffic in armaments have all been charged to the corporate quest for profit.[7]

Complex and important moral issues thus envelop the activities of multinational corporations. The parties to multinational commerce, whether governments or corporations, have been less than exemplary in their conduct. With complexity of this magnitude, it will not suffice simply to assign blame or seek to apportion responsibilities and duties to the various agents of international commerce. It is essential to understand the circumstances in which these difficulties have arisen and to determine what the circumstances will allow. This point is emphasized by the evidence of the past few years, which shows that those involved have gradually become more sensitive and responsible, are moving toward a consensus on standards of conduct in some areas, and are working fitfully to establish the institutions necessary to refine and support these standards. Rancor and confusion remain, of course, but there has also been progress.

The picture of moral endeavor developed in this work is neither static nor abstracted from the uncertainties and limitations of human life. In particular, the sphere of international commerce contains an ethics in evolution. Intense global trade and the problems associated with it burst on the world scene less than a half-century ago. Those involved, given time, have begun to understand what they were about, begun to address areas of difficulty and begun to construct institutional mechanisms to cope with them. If the participants had more closely resembled selfless and purely rational autonomous beings, and if the conditions of international commerce more closely resembled those of a moral Utopia, the problems of multinational commerce would perhaps have been seen much earlier and addressed more decisively. As it happens, human beings and human circumstances fall short of these ideals. The human participants have begun to address these difficult issues only gradually, and the institutions required to support and nurture moral sensitivity in the sphere of international commerce have been equally slow to emerge.

Nonetheless, a higher standard of moral accountability may be demanded at present than would have been feasible a few decades ago. As the circumstances of international commerce stabilize, it is possible that a higher standard may reasonably be sought a few years hence.

This does not imply that actions of the past, present or future are beyond moral criticism. It can always be claimed that circumstances allow a higher or broader scope of moral accountability than those involved in fact displayed. But it remains true that context puts an outer boundary on what may be demanded and shapes the responses that are feasible.

As the title of this work implies, the following analysis will focus on moral issues which are entangled with the existence and activity of multinational corporations. It will not presume that they are the major causal factors in bringing these problems about. Multinational corporations are only one facet of the larger process of economic globalization. Often the problems associated with corporate endeavor can only be understood as part of this larger process and as shaped by it. Furthermore, host and home nations are not simply passive victims or imperialistic aggressors. Reality is far more complex than that, as illustrated by the fact that the United States, which is the home nation for the majority of multinational corporations, is also the *host* of more foreign ventures than any other nation in the world save Canada, and continues to attract foreign investment at ever-increasing rates.[8] Finally, in the past much attention has been devoted to the difficulties caused for developing countries by the endeavors of avaricious multinational enterprise. While poorer nations have often suffered as a result of this globalization, they have also discovered resources for coping and have unearthed important benefits of development and the infusion of capital which can be gained from the attentions of multinational concerns.

Advanced industrialized nations have claimed to be victimized by multinational enterprise as often and as loudly as the outraged governments of developing nations. Moreover, the complexity of these issues is such that multinational corporations are occasionally portrayed as victims rather than manipulators. They are sometimes caught in the middle when governments wage economic warfare on one another, as with US efforts to remove General Noriega from power in Panama, European and American economic sanctions directed against South Africa, or the Arab Oil Embargo of 1973. It has been claimed as well that multinational corporations may become the tools of the imperialistic aspirations of governments, and they sometimes make great commitments of capital and human expertise over substantial periods of time only to be summarily evicted from a nation.[9]

A competent analysis of the moral issues attending multinational commerce must therefore acknowledge the roles and resources of all participants as well as the complex ways in which they interact. Moreover, the analyses of this work will not presume that multinational corporations must inevitably accept primary responsibility for devising adequate remedies. Sometimes they should do so, but on other occasions governments or international bureaucracies will be the best and most appropriate agents of response.

The first step toward an adequate grasp of this complexity is to recognize that multinational corporate endeavor has passed through a number of distinct stages. At each stage its nature, difficulties and hazards have taken different forms. The great confusion and uncertainty swirling around the activities of multinational corporations is due in part to the fact that this activity has taken different shapes at different times.

THE EVOLUTION OF MULTINATIONAL COMMERCE

Immediately following the Second World War, much of the world was a shattered, burned-out shell. The United States was among the few nations left unscathed and found itself overwhelmingly dominant militarily, politically and economically. At that time the American government adopted a policy of strongly encouraging US companies to invest and expand in other parts of the world. Its motivation was both benevolent and ideological.[10] Corporate activity abroad seemed an excellent means of encouraging development and reconstruction in the rest of the world. This was to occur directly via the endeavors of the corporations themselves and indirectly through the example and incentive they provided for others. But policy makers were also powerfully swayed by the motive of spreading the gospel of free enterprise and the benefits of capitalism to the world at large, which was felt to be ready to receive the message.

Without the impetus provided by the American government and the unique circumstances of the immediate post-war era, the surge of multinational corporate activity would quite probably have occurred anyway, though not perhaps so soon or in the form that it did. The shattering developments in communications and transportation of that period would eventually have made the feasibility of such endeavor apparent to all, even to normally parochial Americans. As it happened, however, the first blush of post war multinational corporate activity was overwhelmingly dominated by American firms, and they remain predominant to this day. Because this endeavor was strongly encouraged and coordinated by the American government, corpora-

Introduction 5

tions and government were closely identified by those in many host nations. Hence the rest of the world came to view multinational enterprise as American activity, and American corporations were seen as working hand-in-glove with the US government for mutual benefit.[11] In fact, corporations were seen by many as the *agents* of the US government abroad, serving as instruments of American domination. This perception was underscored and given credence by the enormous disparity in power and wealth separating those corporations from the nations where they functioned. In those days even European nations were ill-equipped to negotiate on equal terms with American commercial interests. Thus arose the perception of great disparities in strength between host countries and their corporate guests, a perception strongly supported by the reality of the day and heightened by the indifference with which corporations sometimes viewed host country needs and sensibilities.

However, the conditions of multinational corporate endeavor soon changed. By the 1960s, many American corporations had developed a taste for multinational activity and happily sought new avenues of investment even without the urgings of the US government.[12] Increased numbers of American corporations found opportunities in the international arena, and (more importantly perhaps) recovering Europe and Japan began to dispatch companies and investment abroad as well.

These developments helped alter the common perception of multinational corporations and their activities. It no longer seemed that multinational corporations exclusively served the mercantilist interests of one nation, the United States. Corporate actors from a variety of nations emerged, each competing for a share of global commerce. Furthermore, as corporations developed an appetite for international commerce, they learned to free themselves from the effective control of *both* host *and* home nations. They were able to threaten the interests of home nations by, for example, moving capital elsewhere or combing foreign nations for cheap labor. They also learned to evade legal control in host nations and reduce tax burdens by deftly shifting operations and book-keeping arrangements from nation to nation.

During this period, in other words, multinational corporations came to be seen as independent operators who were not only free of the control of nation-states but able to use their powers and resources to threaten governmental sovereignty in pursuit of their commercial interests.[13]

Following the 1960s, however, the picture was transformed once again. With increasing numbers of corporations from widely differing nations seeking opportunity abroad, host nations discovered they were able to gain advantage for themselves by pitting competing corporations against one another. Further, host nations found that the legal and military perquisites of national sovereignty could be wielded to force corporations into the service of their interests. The outright threat of nationalization was only the crudest and most spectacular of these instruments. Other, more subtle, means of control included manipulating laws regulating corporate activity or forcefully demanding renegotiation of existing contracts.

In due course the embattled militancy of many host nations also played its role. This militancy was in part a reaction to the arrogance, callousness and clumsiness too often displayed by corporations in the early years of post-war international commerce. But national militancy was due also to the identification of multinational corporations with the perceived imperialism of their home nations, so they became latter-day symbols of colonial domination. Hostility was also fed by the very strong desire of developing nations to establish themselves as sovereign and independent states who were masters of their own affairs and free from external manipulation.

This militancy put multinational corporations on the defensive, but corporate vulnerability was heightened by their own changed perceptions. They became sensitive to charges of neo-colonialism and, concurrently, their accumulating experience gave them increased sympathy for the particular needs, desires and perspectives of nations where they sought to do business.[14] They had, in other words, lost some of the arrogant self-assurance of earlier years. But a more consequential change was the recognition that they were able to conduct business and reap healthy profits even when subject to close regulation by host nations and when the terms of agreement were clearly designed to serve national goals of economic development.[15] The dogma that corporations could function only under conditions of unfettered commercial freedom weakened.

By the end of the 1970s, in other words, multinational corporations were commonly portrayed as helpless giants who could be harnessed by militant host nations in the service of their political and economic goals.[16] Advanced industrialized nations came increasingly to fear that their own corporations might be captured by host nations and wheeled round to be used against them.

The picture of the present day has changed yet again and is much less clearly defined than those of earlier periods. Developing host nations have generally subdued their militancy and come to recognize not only that the activities of multinational corporations can be managed for national benefit but that the infusion of capital they bring is necessary for continued economic progress; thus developing nations have often reversed earlier positions and are now actively seeking the attentions of multinational corporations.[17]

Home nations, for their part, are increasingly impressed by the realization that they are becoming part of one global economy. Their predominant response is to accept the inevitable and they are, as a result, creating the institutions and mechanisms necessary to support this integration. They appear destined to establish this global economy on principles of free trade, in part because this is the only basis on which all participants are likely to agree.

Corporations have found themselves in more intense competition as more players enter the fray, and the players are increasingly coming to include participants from developing nations that were once only hosts of international corporate endeavor. Corporate enterprises have also learned to be more flexible. They have learned they can function under strict regulation by host nations, and have often found it convenient to enter into local alliances and agreements with erstwhile competitors.[18] They have shown themselves to be increasingly sympathetic to the aspirations of their host nations and have not, at least in principle, vetoed the establishment of a global code of conduct for corporations.[19] More to the point, they have had the idea thrust upon them, as the result of public outcry over corporate activity in South Africa, that their moral sensitivity must sometimes range beyond the narrow confines of commercial endeavor.

The present may be characterized as an era of wary realism on the part of all parties, combined with a heightened sense of their limitations and a recognition of the legitimacy of the perspectives and aspirations of other participants. Indeed, all find themselves working haphazardly to establish the foundations for a global economy, an undertaking that will loom increasingly large in coming years.[20]

A MATURE MORAL ORDER

One general claim of the present work is that the various parties active in international commerce have been groping toward what can be termed a 'mature moral order'. In a mature moral order the members of a community have a distinct sense of accepted standards of conduct; are aware of how responsibility and accountability are assigned to participants; understand that there are effective sanctions for use against those who fail to uphold recognized standards; acknowledge that there are means of recognizing those whose conduct is exemplary; and, most importantly, collectively recognize that they are part of a *moral* enterprise.

The above is not a conception of an ideal moral condition; mature moral orders may be deficient in various ways. Their standards may be open to criticism, their membership may be overly restricted, or their mechanisms of enforcement and reward may function mechanically and awkwardly. At least for Western European thought, the moral ideal would be something like Kant's kingdom of ends, where each participant is fully rational, completely selfless, fully committed to performing his or her duty, freely motivated to do so and, finally, in complete agreement on the norms of moral conduct. A mature moral order approximates to the Kantian kingdom of ends in a number of ways and may plausibly be construed as the kingdom of ends suitably modified for the limitations of the real world and actual human beings.

Nonetheless, a mature moral order is *morally* preferable to moral anarchy and, usually, to patterns of conduct which only approximate to it. It is morally preferable because agents under its influence are more likely to have a clearly delineated sense of moral responsibility and to express this sensitivity in action. Also, moral patients (those affected by others' conduct) are more likely to have a clear sense of what is due to them *and* the belief that the community as a whole will support their efforts to be treated correctly. In other words, good is more likely to be done and evil more likely avoided with a mature moral order in place.

A mature moral order will be embedded in a particular human context. It may evolve when human beings see themselves as members of a distinct group and understand that their activities within it are morally significant. Because a mature moral order is thus context-dependent, it may be thrown into disarray with changes in the structure of its society. Several decades ago, for example, American practices regulating marriage, and relations between the sexes generally, were thrown into disarray when American family life changed.

When a new arena of human activity opens, there may be disarray until a mature moral order, or its approximation, can develop. A new arena of of this type emerged with the advent of intense international commerce, and of the multinational corporation, following the Second World War. The participants, both corporations and governments, were fresh on the scene, and the full implications of what they were creating were not apparent (indeed, could not be apparent given the flux and novelty of the period). Furthermore, there was as yet no sense of community uniting those in the arena of international commerce, none of the shared practices on which a community could be built, and no clear appreciation of the ways in which their activity was having a morally significant impact on people's lives.

Specific moral practices may approach more or less closely to the mature. They may have some of its features or have them to a greater or lesser degree. But there is nothing inevitable about the evolution of this sort of system. Where there is rapid turn-over of participants, where conditions are so desperate that survival is always the main goal, or where there is no settled institutional structure to support it, a mature moral order may fail to develop. There are signs that the arena of international commerce is gradually approaching such a system although, again, there is nothing foreordained about this evolution.

Some features of a mature moral order are already present in international commerce, if only to a degree. Most importantly, there is an emerging awareness that distinctly moral problems are entangled among the activities of multinational corporations. Also there are halting efforts to establish generally acknowledged standards of conduct for those involved. These attempts are currently in hiatus and are marred by disagreement over whether they should be mandatory for corporate enterprises and governments or whether they should be voluntary.[21] But it is significant that the attempts are being made and that the need for them is acknowledged. Another sign of progress toward the development of a mature moral system is that the various parties (that is, home nations, host nations and the corporations themselves) have begun to recognize that they are members of a single community. They confer with one another, devise agreements and discuss matters of mutual concern. There are also institutions, most particularly the World Bank, the International Monetary Fund (IMF) and the General Agreement on Tariffs and Trade (GATT), that have substantial influence on the shape and flow of international commerce. Though their concerns do not specifically include those of moral equity, they are helping to create the sort of stable community necessary to support a well-developed sense of moral accountability. The United Nations has served as a forum for airing moral concerns and establishing some of the institutional machinery needed to meet problems generated by the present intense level of multinational commerce. It seems likely to find a larger and more effective role in future years.

Present circumstances of multinational commerce still fall distinctly short of a mature moral order. Among these lapses are the absence of clearly established and authoritative proceedures to identify those who breach standards or to initiate remedial action. Neither are there means to acknowledge or reward those whose conduct is exemplary. Further, the evolution of a genuine international moral community of commercial activity is hampered by the great flux of participants. New corporations enter the arena daily, new nations come to participate either as host or as home nations, and the roles of the various parties alter from year to year. Many, such as the United States, Canada and Great Britain, are *both* host *and* home nations. Others, including South Korea and India, have primarily been host nations in the past but are increasingly active as home nations of vigorous multinational corporations.[22] This flux and the possibility that the continued expansion of global commerce will reveal yet more difficulties make claims about future developments a hazardous enterprise. Nonetheless, even if current portents turn out to be misleading or illusory, it will remain worthwhile to continue examination of the economic homogenization of the globe, since humanity will not be able to avoid coming to terms with it.

PLAN OF THE CHAPTERS

The work of the remainder of this project is twofold: to examine the circumstances and agents of international commerce, and then to examine the major types of moral issues that have arisen as the result of international commerce and the shapes it has taken. Issues which are unique to the activities of multinational corporations and the circumstances of international commerce will receive the greatest attention, though there will necessarily be areas of overlap with problems of strictly domestic corporate activity.

The first two chapters will formulate its normative basis. Chapters 1 and 2 will thus address issues and problems of moral accountability in the context of international commerce and formulate the normative principles to be used for future analysis. Each following chapter will examine a particular arena of moral difficulty involving multinational corporations. Hence, Chapter 3 will focus on problems resulting from the size and power of multinational corporations, while Chapter 4 will examine difficulties arising from the cultural and economic diversity of the various parts of the world where multinationals conduct business.

Chapter 5 deals with issues of mobility, the ease with which multinational corporations move products, labor, capital and bookkeeping operations from nation to nation or arrange their affairs in such a fashion that it will be unclear which governments have jurisdiction over them. Chapter 6 focuses on a different sort of problem, that of the facility with which corporations may be manipulated by governments to suit their own political purposes. Corporate entanglement in arms trade and economic embargoes are salient examples. Multinational corporations are heavily involved in South Africa and deeply enmeshed in controversy over this presence. Chapter 7 will examine these matters, which provide vivid examples of issues in which multinational corporations play a significant role and which the world clearly recognizes as moral difficulties. The concluding chapter will sketch the extent to which moral sensitivity may be legitimately demanded of multinational corporations and national governments at the present time. It will also look to the future to see how the circumstances of moral accountability may evolve and what steps may be taken to direct this evolution in more, rather than less, humane directions.

1 Corporate Moral Accountability

This chapter's topic may be dazedly unrealistic. It is possible that there are decisive reasons for believing that corporations cannot be expected to shoulder more than minimal moral responsibility. The arguments undergirding this view take several different forms and have varying implications. One is that corporations are not the sort of entities that can be moral agents.[1] Another is the claim that the perpetual struggle for survival and the pressures of competition preclude any moral scruple other than the grim commitment to prevail.[2] A related argument is that corporate officers have a solemn duty to seek profits above all else and are irresponsible and presumptuous if they fail to do so.[3] A final, more modest, argument is that corporations are not capable of unilaterally adopting moral scruples and that persons within them cannot accept moral responsiblity beyond that delineated by their corporate role.[4] These claims will be considered in turn. While each encapsulates important truth, none, as will be seen, is sufficient to preclude moral scruple altogether.

The following discussions address the nature and circumstances of *all* corporations, not only multinational enterprises. Commercial activity in the international arena does not qualitatively change the nature of corporate moral agency or the conditions of moral sensitivity. However, the present circumstances of multinational commerce are such that moral difficulties are apt to be present in more intense and less manageable fashion than on the domestic level.

For one thing, the regulatory agencies and legal strictures that order commercial activity within nations exist in only fragmentary and tenuous fashion on the international level. Indeed, their ability to evade effective governmental control is one of the disgruntling talents multinational corporations possess. One result is that corporations may have a less vivid sense that standards of commercial activity exist. Another is that those who are unscrupulous or irresponsible are more likely to escape unscathed or undetected. Furthermore, the size, complexity and geographic dispersal that generally accompany multinational endeavor make it less likely that individuals within these enterprises will have a clear sense of what corporations, or their subsidiaries, are doing or how they affect human life.[5] Large size and daunting complexity also decrease the probability that any given individual will have explicit responsibility to address moral difficulty. Finally, the cultural, economic and political diversity which attend the operations of multinational corporations increase the likelihood that harm will be caused unknowingly, that enterprises will find themselves in collaboration with unsavory political groups or that their activities will clash with local cultural norms.

The moral context is more treacherous on the international level, but the arguments of this and other chapters seek to demonstrate that its complexities do not forestall moral sensitivity altogether. Certainly it would be shortsighted to expect the same standards of moral accountability in the present arena of international commerce that could be demanded with a mature moral order in place. Because there is only a nascent moral order, there will be less clarity on standards, greater likelihood that abuses will occur and go unpunished, more chance that participants will lack a clear sense of moral accountability, and a greater probability that moral compromises and half-measures must be accepted.

CORPORATE MORAL AGENCY

The reluctance to view corporations as moral agents can partly be traced to the fact that they, like other institutions, are starkly different from those traditionally considered moral agents. Western European thought attributes moral guilt, responsibility or merit to the discrete human individual. This is because the single individual obviously possesses rationality, consciousness, the ability to make decisions and then act on them, and, most importantly, the ability to select principles of conduct to guide decisions. Persons deficient in any of these are not deemed full moral agents. Infants, not yet fully rational and still undisciplined, are not moral agents; neither are those who have lost the ability to reason or control their physical movements; nor are those who are 'brainwashed' or thoroughly manipulated by others.

Institutions are not organic wholes then in the manner of human persons. Rather, they are collections of distinct individuals who are related to one another and to the larger world by means of defined roles and fixed institutional structure. Corporate 'actions' are thus the coordinated actions of various persons, or they are artificial actions, such as offering stock, selling subsidiaries or corporate reorganization, which are made possible by shared human conventions. Enterprises are not capable of the smooth, fully integrated exertions of single individuals, though the more highly developed and effective such institutions become, the closer they will approach this ideal of unified, organic function. Furthermore, it would be most awkward to claim that human institutions are conscious in the manner of human agents or that they 'think' as persons do. However, they have the ability to take in information, analyze it, then respond to it. While it stretches language and thought to call them 'conscious', they are said to be 'aware' and to 'react'. Also, they are spoken of as taking action or as being rational or irrational. They certainly choose among courses of action, possess mechanisms for selecting one rather than others, and make these decisions in rational or irrational fashion. But notice that this awareness, this freedom and this rationality are dependent on the freedom and rationality of those single human beings who compose them. Corporate abilities are therefore derivative.

This result does not imply that corporate activity is merely complex individual activity. Corporations are not simply haphazard arrays of human individuals, as those massed at a bus stop or enjoying a public park on a sunny afternoon would be. Individuals within corporations are connected to one another by an organizational structure which defines roles for them, specifies the ways these roles relate to those of others, and contains mechanisms for deliberating, making decisions and performing actions.

Structures of this sort enable the corporation as a whole to take action in a manner which is distinct from the massed actions of the individuals within it. Its undertakings are not, in other words, merely the summed total of individual acts but are structured to allow specific patterns of decision and action. Individuals within them could not function in the manner they do without the corporate structure. But the structure also *forestalls* some acts: those outside the specified range of activity for individuals within them, those opposed to its policies or those not supported by the acts or permissions of other members of the larger stucture. Corporate structure markedly restructures the agency of those individual persons who function within it.

Corporations, therefore, have the qualities required for moral agency, though in less elegant and more complex fashion than single human individuals. They are, in other words, able to control their actions and make rational rather than irrational decisions. Because they nearly always possess a spectrum of possible actions and are capable of making reasoned choices among them, they can be held morally accountable for those they select.

However, corporate accountability differs from that of individual persons. When an individual goes astray, that person *as a whole* is morally wrong and blameworthy, but corporations are far more complex. Only the Henry Fords of commerce and industry, the corporate patriarchs, possess the sort of close relationship between individual and corporate entity that allows the moral accountability of the one and the other to coincide. For all other corporations and all other persons within them, accountability must be apportioned in complex fashion. Individuals within corporations have different ranges of authority and responsibility, and these ranges are closely defined. Chief executive officers have wide bands of responsibility, and therefore considerable ability to direct corporate activity and concerns. But they remain employees, rather than corporate patriarchs, accountable to stockholders and required to follow the general policies of the corporation. In addition, they are not likely to undertake action successfully which is not widely supported by other corporate officials. Lesser employees will have narrower ranges of authority and find their freedom of action more closely circumscribed by the requirement that their efforts mesh smoothly with those of others in the corporate hierarchy. However, any of these persons may feel morally accountable in ways not clearly delineated by corporate structure, or they may find that corporate policy or the undertakings of the larger entity are morally amiss or not sufficiently morally sensitive. In such cases the individual may feel both frustrated and helpless. Yet, as later discussion will show, their dilemma is not altogether hopeless. And, because corporations differ from individuals, the accountability of the corporate whole will differ from that of any particular individual within it. Whole corporate entities, for example, commonly pledge to uphold moral standards, or have standards thrust upon them by others, such as stockholders' groups or governments.

The contention that corporations are moral agents is supported by the fact that corporations clearly are held accountable in many ways: for instance, by their stockholders, regulative agencies and legal statute. If they fail to meet the various standards established by these parties, there are means for seeking out those responsible and gaining redress. Furthermore, corporations themselves commonly acknowledge a distinct sense of *moral* responsibility when dealing with employees and in their external business transactions.[6] Of course, there are occasional failings, but these are explicitly recognized as moral failures. There are cases, in addition, where corporations embark on courses of action which they are not legally required to perform, spurred by their avowed sense of moral responsibility.[7]

It is entirely possible that these actions are sometimes hypocritical. It is certainly true that the appearance of integrity is sometimes forced on corporations by the pressures of competition or the demands of corporate image. Moral rectitude can nearly always be explained in terms of self-interest of one sort or another. The important point, however, is that hypocrisy of this sort acknowledges the legitimacy and relevance of moral scruple. Nonetheless, even if corporations have the attributes of moral agency and occasionally embrace moral scruple, it is possible that these are merely superficial froth. Perhaps, in other words, the pressures of competition and efforts to survive make pronouncements of moral scruple necessarily ephemeral.

THE HOBBESIAN SITUATION

The primal fact of corporate life is that enterprises must grow and seek profits or die. Corporations that fail to move into new or promising markets, fail to take full advantage of occasions for profitable activity, retreat from fruitful markets, or engage in inefficient practices (those, that is, more costly than available alternatives), leave the field open to their competitors who may be more aggressive and less scrupulous. In business, furthermore, bigger is generally better, because 'bigger' implies more resources, more expertise, more options; more power, in short, which translates into increased ability to fend off or dominate competitors. So, the argument goes, the fact of competition drives corporations, as a matter of life or death, to seek profits and growth. It is vitally important under these conditions to avoid any disadvantage which may diminish or neutralize competitiveness.

This argument is a restatement, in the corporate context, of Thomas Hobbes's argument regarding mortal competition in the state of nature. In both the Hobbesian state of nature and the arena of corporate activity there is intense competition, where competitors are forced into conflict by the pressures of circumstance, and where the stakes of conflict are life and death. Applied to persons, the Hobbesian analysis stipulates that individuals must seek to escape the state of nature in an attempt to avoid perpetual mortal conflict. Hence, individuals founded the state in the hope that it would ease their burden of self-preservation. But corporate existence is not protected by higher authority. On the contrary, mortal competition is its very essence. The basic ideology of capitalist endeavor mandates that competition should be free and fair; in other words, that no participant will be able to escape it. Insofar as Hobbes's argument requires inescapable competition, it describes corporate activity more closely than the circumstances of individual persons.

However, corporations – as claimed earlier – are persons only in an artificial sense, as is talk of corporate flourishing or death. Only persons have a strong claim to life and hence to a right of self-defense as the means to preserve it. Just as the faculties of rationality, awareness and freedom derive from those of individual persons, the moral claims of institutions, including corporations, to survival or well-being are derivative in the sense that whatever claims they have to existence or well-being must depend in some way on the existence and well-being of individual persons. Governments of nation-states, for example, have a claim to a right of self-defense only in the second-hand sense that their continued existence may sometimes be necessary to preserve the lives of human individuals. Corporations cannot claim even this much, as it is rare for anyone's life to be endangered when a corporation succumbs.

It is true, however, that corporations, particularly very large ones, hold responsibility for the well-being of large numbers of persons: employees, stockholders, suppliers and dependents. Such ties give their survival substantial moral weight, moral weight that will be *out*weighed only in extraordinary circumstances. Nevertheless, it is rare for managers to be faced with a single, stark choice between corporate survival and dissolution. Choices of this sort, furthermore (where corporate survival will be morally outweighed by other factors), will be less frequent still. When such occasions do arise, it will be apparent to all that those involved are faced with difficult and tragic choices, not routine ones, as where a corporation has invested heavily in a new drug which, shortly before it is to be released to the public, is discovered to be dangerous to human life.

In advanced industrialized nations (those most likely to spawn multinational corporations), the demise of a corporation is not as tragic as may initially appear. 'Non-survival' generally means going bankrupt and being reorganized, being managed by trustees or being bought out by another corporation. It rarely entails the total dissolution of the corporate organism, along with its jobs and resources. Hence the death of a corporation is not at all like the death of a human being or the destruction of a nation. Partly because competition is a matter of corporate life and death, and these are normal occurrences, societies have developed mechanisms to cope with these vicissitudes which are engineered to make corporate death minimally disruptive.[8]

What is more, corporations normally have a variety of opportunities for profitable endeavor. They are able to select some and cultivate others but do not often find themselves in situations where survival competes directly with moral scruple, since profits can be sought in different avenues.Furthermore, international corporations can normally afford to lose money on at least some ventures without endangering their survival. Taking gambles, and sometimes losing, is a normal part of business activity, and thus an eventuality which corporations are generally well equipped to face. When there is no need to choose between corporate survival and moral scruple, managers cannot claim that there is no room for moral accountability in corporate activity.

The argument from Hobbesian mortal competition also skirts another facet of corporate activity. Corporations, even bitter competitors, routinely communicate and cooperate in a variety of ways. They are thus quite unlike Hobbesian rivals in the state of nature. Corporations that are direct competitors in some areas occasionally find it useful to cooperate closely in others. General Motors (GM) and Toyota, for instance, bitter rivals in many ways, have found it convenient to undertake several joint ventures, including an auto assembly plant in California.[9] Unlike Hobbesian competitors in the state of nature, corporate competitors *are* able to communicate and initiate joint planning and shared ventures. The implication for moral accountability is that corporations need not act in solitary, *ad hoc* fashion but may work with others to address moral problems jointly.[10] This is not to say that difficult moral issues can be resolved easily or without long-term effort. It is only that they are generally manageable, given good-will and reasonable persistence.

THE OBLIGATION TO SEEK PROFITS

The Hobbesian argument from mortal competition cannot therefore demonstrate that there is no rational place for moral scruple in the decisions of corporate leaders of multinational concerns. However, there will occasionally be cases where moral scruple directly conflicts with corporate profitability. When such instances arise, even morally sensitive managers may feel strongly compelled by their obligation, owed to stockholders and fellow employees, to seek profits. As argued in the next chapter, special responsibilities of this sort are both legitimate and important. It is clearly worthwhile that people be able to accept special responsibilities in their dealings with others and that they accord them significant weight.

Without questioning the moral validity of capitalism itself, there is little reason to believe that the special responsibilities of corporate managers should normally be of lesser account than any of the other special responsibilities human beings legitimately accept. Given the range of consequences corporate endeavor generates for human life and well-being, these responsibilities will have considerable weight; more weight perhaps than some arrays of special responsibility, yet less than others. The special responsibility of political leaders for the lives and well-being of the people of an entire nation, for example, would be greater.

Though corporate responsibilities are important, they are not of all-consuming importance. Given circumstances of sufficient gravity, they will be overridden, as when the specific duty to seek profits conflicts directly with the general duty all individual persons have to preserve human life. The present work, in other words, does not deny the validity of arguments that corporate officers have special duties to seek profits, and neither does it deny the moral significance of these duties. What it does deny is that such duties are absolute and overriding on any and all occasions.

CORPORATE MORAL INITIATIVE

The above arguments aside, however, another awaits. The claim may be that corporations cannot develop effective moral sensibilities and moral standards which they do not already possess. This argument is a certain kind of claim about feasibility. It is not the abstract, theoretical argument examined earlier about how corporations are not in any sense capable of being agents. Rather, it is more a practical argument about the ways in which corporations must operate. It is the claim that, where corporations do not already possess particular types of moral sensibility, they will not be able to develop them. The core of the problem is, as pointed out earlier, that the institution does not operate as an organic whole. Its functioning results from the activity of various individuals, working together in ways shaped by their corporate roles.

For example, as a private individual the Chairman of GM, could not announce GM's withdrawal from its operations in South Africa.[11] He could only undertake this action via his corporate role as Chairman and *then* only insofar as he abided by the constraints and procedures which define it. In part, this is due to the fact that corporate activity is rarely the single act of a particular individual. It is normally the result of the combined actions of numbers of individuals which must mesh in well-orchestrated ways for corporate undertakings to occur. Institutional roles define and establish these various ways of interlocking and reinforcing. Where the roles are not followed or when the acts of one individual do not mesh with those of others, corporate action cannot take place, and the system will stall. The general claim, then, is that this system of interlocking roles does not allow the introduction of moral constraint where it has previously been absent, since individuals within the institution *cannot* act contrary to, or outside, their pre-established roles and these *must* merge smoothly with the acts of others.

The moral problems encountered here are of two types. One is that of the 'whistleblowers', those who seek to combat cases where corporations fail to uphold standards which they have officially adopted.[12] The second type of problem is where individuals seek to expand the range of corporate moral accountability, by perhaps lobbying for policies which strongly support the rights of the underprivileged or which are committed to environmental purity.

It is not difficult to understand how the constraints of institutional action create difficulty for would-be whistleblowers. The actions of concerned individuals, to make a difference, must usually hew to the contours of their roles and mesh with the established sensibilities of others surrounding and above them. Where their concerns do not mesh with established institutional structure, as they do not in attempts at whistleblowing, it may be nearly impossible for the institution as a whole to be sensitive or respond gracefully. Consequently, concerned individuals may be compelled to step outside their institutional roles, and perhaps entirely outside the institutional structure itself, to make themselves heard. Only the most determined and resourceful individual – and the most fortuituous combination of circumstances – will make a significant difference in conditions of this sort. Such responses will not be routine features of institutional operation, and they cannot be the expected reactions of ordinary individuals. While examples of moral heroism are not totally beyond the realm of the possible, they are distinctly uncommon, and it is easy to see why it is argued that institutions cannot be expected to be sensitive in these matters.

This does not demonstrate, however, that efforts to respond to moral shortcomings will be impossible for all people in all situations. There *are* examples of heroic people who have successfully combated moral abuses in corporations. However, some members of corporate hierarchies are better placed for such endeavors than others, and some persons will be better equipped in personal resources to speak out and press for change than others. But even ordinary people, with ordinary allotments of courage and self-confidence, may be moved to act where moral problems are sufficiently compelling. The engineers at Morton Thiokol who sought to halt the disastrous flight of the Challenger space shuttle in 1986 may have been ordinary in these ways[13] yet, where they could see that human lives were clearly endangered, they were willing to press their worries.

Furthermore, the above complications do not entail that it is impossible to alter institutional structures to encourage morally responsible conduct. All well-managed corporations have ways of eliciting the sorts of behavior they desire. They have the means, in other words, to encourage certain types of behavior in ordinary, neither saintly nor heroic, persons and not leave matters to the occasional exceptional individual. Corporations have the wherewithal to emphasize that moral concerns are welcomed and will receive a thorough hearing. They can establish avenues for making complaints, protecting anonymity, ensuring that concerns will be heard by those with sufficient authority to respond, *and* by demonstrating public support and appreciation for those who reveal moral problems.[14] The latter point cannot be overemphasized. If the concern is with ordinary people, who have ordinary intelligence, determination and self-confidence, it is clear that they need to be encouraged to act in a morally responsible fashion and to understand explicitly that such conduct is approved and appreciated. The saintly or heroic may not require such inducements, but plain persons most emphatically do.

There are also a number of mechanisms for allowing corporations to alter or extend the range of moral standards they uphold. In publicly owned corporations, for example, it has sometimes been the case that groups of stockholders have pressed for change. Stockholders are often ordinary people with ordinary moral sensibilities but are free of the internal constraints of corporate structure. They are not, furthermore, employees whose jobs are controlled by the corporation and therefore under pressure to accept the restraints it establishes. Where they have special concerns or where their consciences have been pricked, stockholders have sometimes been willing to voice them and make efforts to incorporate moral scruple into corporate policy. Since they are owners and since their investments are at stake, they have the privilege of restraining their desire for profits by concerns of moral scruple in ways that hired managers may not. Corporations, for example, have been pressed by their stockholders to alter their policies in South Africa.[15] In addition, there exist investment firms that develop portfolios designed to reflect the moral sensibilities of investors as well as the more traditional concerns of profitability.[16]

Corporate managers also have the means to bring issues of moral concern to the attention of stockholders and seek change. Professional managers have few qualms about voicing corporate interest in other areas, such as tax laws or trade regulation. They do not hesitate to establish venues to air these concerns or to seek to generate interest for them among stockholders or others. They have the instruments to accomplish the same in the area of moral scruple, should they be moved to do so.

Before this point, or if corporate employees reside deeper in the corporate hierarchy, it is frequently possible simply to raise issues of moral concern for discussion and reflection within the corporation. Obviously, some will be better placed than others both in terms of personal qualities of self-confidence and persistence and in terms of their position within the institution to establish this focus of attention. But such efforts are not absolutely out of the question.

As with other moral issues, there is often benefit even where initial efforts are unsuccessful. Simply raising an issue to consciousness can be one step along the way to creating a climate of opinion where further change will become possible, or an unsuccessful outcry in response to one particular incident may dampen the prospect of future occurrences. The timing and mode of presentation can be important features of such efforts. The Watergate scandal of the Nixon administration was a prolonged morality drama which had the effect of making moral concerns legitimate for hard-headed, clear-thinking adults in the United States. Seizing the atmosphere of interest generated by scandal can often be an effective step to making moral concerns credible.[17]

In sum, corporations have the attributes of freedom and rationality required for moral agency. This agency is more complex in its nature and distribution than that of individual human beings. Nonetheless, careful analysis reveals ways in which this agency is distributed among the particular human beings holding various positions within an institution. Were a mature moral order in place, moral responsibilities would be defined and distributed in explicit and orderly fashion, so that each participant knew clearly what obligation and authority he or she possessed and this was publicly acknowledged both within corporations and by those outside. This applies to corporations whose operations are solely domestic and those whose endeavors range more broadly. However, the complexity and uncertainty presently endemic to the arena of international commerce intensify and magnify these difficulties. As matters stand, there are no explicit mechanisms of this sort and no such common understanding. Thus the analysis of the present work reveals only the feasibility and possible shape of such accountability. It shows that it is not impossible for those within corporations to shoulder such responsibility but acknowledges that the form this takes and prospects for success must be determined by their role and perquisites within the structure. Moral activism under present circumstances must, in other words, be more difficult and require more personal initiative and courage than under a mature moral order, but it is not impossible.

Furthermore, the duties of corporate officers to seek profits, the pressures of competition and the demands of corporate survival do not absolutely rule out broader moral sensitivity. These concerns have moral weight but sometimes they will be outweighed by other concerns *and* a variety of courses of moral action may be undertaken which will be compatible with their stern discipline. Further, as will be emphasized in succeeding chapters, it is important to acknowledge that the demands of moral accountability can frequently be met in creative and flexible fashion. Simplistic ideas of the requirements of moral success, the claim that moral scruple always makes absolute, all-or-nothing demands of perfection, must be avoided.

It remains to determine the sort of moral principles best suited to guide corporate endeavor and the accommodations which must be made to suit them to the particular status of multinational corporations in the international arena. It is necessary as well to devise a schema of analysis to structure the examination of particular moral issues and reveal avenues of response. Both the above must be grounded on a specific normative perspective. This last must, therefore, be the first task of the following chapter, with treatments of the other topics to follow.

2 Structure of Response

Moral claims must be grounded on a normative perspective. Current philosophical discussion offers several candidates for this foundation, including intuitionism, virtue-based ethics of various stripes, several varieties of rights theories and, finally, utilitarianism. A quick scan of these reveals that an iteration of utilitarian theory is best suited to the requirements of multinational commerce.

THE OPTIONS

Intuitionism is the view that answers to moral questions are found by direct inspection of the normative qualities inhering in practical situations.[1] However, where issues are hotly contested or where there is no consensus on what is morally proper, there are few crevices to provide a toehold for intuitions. The appeal to intuition is most useful where there is a received moral consensus and a stable, well-established social context to support it.[2] The context of international commerce lacks these. Indeed, within a mature moral order intuitions, understood as vivid conceptions of moral propriety and a well-honed sense of when they are transgressed, can be useful and important, but the arena of multinational commerce nowhere approaches that stage.

A second normative perspective which has received some attention recently is that of appeals to moral virtue.[3] But, once again, the appeal to virtue has distinct limitations within the context of international commerce and cannot be the sole springboard of moral analysis. The enterprises engaged in international commerce change from day to day, and the people within them come and go as quickly. There is no stable community able to nurture virtuous activity or refine standards of virtuous conduct. The flux and disorder of international commerce does not, in other words, presently hold the requirements for the cultivation or the practice of virtue.

The appeal to virtue suffers a more basic difficulty, however. To proclaim that people ought to be brave, honest or loyal does not address the question of when and under what conditions the display of these qualities is necessary or admirable. Courage, for example, does not contain its own inertial compass. It must be guided by some distinct normative principle. As Kant understood, misdirected courage or loyalty can do more harm than good.[4] Furthermore, the world presently confronts moral issues which embody genuine moral perplexity: those where the difficulty is not to summon the resources to do what is right, but to determine what moral accountability requires.

As with intuitions, this result does not imply that virtues have no place in a mature moral order. Within a stable mature moral order the conditions requisite for virtue would be present, and a culture of virtue could have an important role in defining and supporting moral accountability. But a culture of virtue must follow the evolution of community rather than precede it. It cannot stand alone.

Nonetheless, individual enterprises may seek to establish a corporate culture in which people are honest or loyal, and several have taken steps to encourage and support behavior of this sort.[5] This also demonstrates that it is possible for corporations to engender other virtues (those of moral courage and initiative, for example), and they should do so. Corporations themselves, as opposed to the people within them, may also seek to develop certain virtues. Various corporations are commonly acknowledged to be exceptionally fair, prudent or honest.[6] These qualities cannot be ascribed to them in the same manner as to individuals, and perhaps the conditions of culture which support virtue for individual persons must change considerably when the effort is made to cultivate them in corporations. But what is possible for individual corporations is not yet feasible for the arena of multinational commerce as a whole. The level of organization and stability which allows a single corporation to engender particular virtues in its employees or to develop them for itself are not available in the international arena. Conditions do not yet allow a general culture of virtue for all participants in international commerce or provide the means to support it.

Appeals to rights have also proliferated in the past several decades and have received the lion's share of attention from philosophers and theoreticians.[7] Rights, however, share a distinctive feature of appeals to virtue. It is that the bare appeal to rights cannot determine what rights people have, whether they have any at all, or how to adjudicate rights in cases of conflict. Thus rights must in turn have a normative foundation, and this has been sought in appeals to rational contract, the requirements of individual autonomy, the fundamental needs of persons, or utilitarianism.[8]

Except for the last, all claim that rights can never be overridden or taken away from persons, and this is avowed to be their decisive advantage. However, this strength also carries weakness, as a quick survey of prominent collections of rights suggests. The UN's Universal Declaration of Human Rights, for example, is simply a roster of goals and the resources which it would be very good for all people to have.[9] The rights of the Universal Declaration are not, in other words, present entitlements which generate obligations. Other conceptions of rights, such as Ronald Dworkin's 'right to equal concern and respect', are so abstract and ethereal as to give little concrete guidance in matters of practice, a feature shared with such claimed entitlements as the individual's right to life or the right to human dignity.[10]

However, when rights are given distinct moral bite, and are delineated sharply enough to introduce genuine constraint, other difficulties emerge. Rights with this degree of specificity will inevitably conflict with one another and with other moral concerns. Means for adjudicating among them must then be sought. There will also be disagreements about just exactly how rights are to be specified on such a concrete level. Furthermore, rights are typically conceived as all-or-nothing entitlements, leaving no room for compromise or half-measures. But there will frequently be occasions when it will be impossible to meet the claims of all holders of rights. When this occurs, it will be necessary to retreat to what Joel Feinberg calls 'the manifesto sense of rights', or to couch them in ever vaguer abstractions, or to attempt some other formulation.[11]

The above problems can be met only within a highly structured social setting, where there are institutional means for determining exactly which rights exist, how they apply to various concrete situations, and how to sustain mechanisms of enforcement and adjudication of conflicts. Rights have an important role to play in human affairs, but they can only work effectively within an organized institutional setting, and they cannot establish their own normative foundation. Quite clearly the present conditions of international commerce, or those of the near future, will not provide such a foundation. Moral accountability on the level of multinational commerce must, for the most part, remain an *ad hoc*, rough and ready affair. The institutional structures being devised do not currently have the authority, the scope, or the judicial machinery required to support a viable system of rights, and a consensus on the normative basis for rights remains to be developed.

In light of the above difficulties, an appeal to some version of utilitarianism holds most promise. It more readily accommodates the flux and disorder of current multinational commerce. It does not require a sophisticated institutional setting to be effective and readily permits half-measures, as well as *ad hoc*, tentative moral floundering. Unlike the salient options, it offers a well-defined normative foundation, that of maximizing good. Utilitarians have diverse views of how to describe this 'good'. The present work, following the lead of R.M. Hare, defines utilitarian good in terms of the preferences people hold, or those which it is reasonable to believe they would hold following reasoned deliberation.[12] While not entirely beyond criticism, this approach has the signal advantage of cutting through much of the mystification surrounding concepts of the good and of encouraging consultation with those human beings who have most at stake when moral judgments must be made. It also has the important value of readily accommodating the widely different cultures, values and ideologies of the world. This is especially important given the absence of any broadly persuasive efforts to discover moral values which exist independently of what people seek. Thus the version of utilitarianism developed here is well suited to cope with the present constraints of multinational commerce.[13]

This approach does not avoid difficulty when applied to the conditions of multinational commerce, unfortunately. Among the vexing issues of moral accountability is the difficulty that people are often harmed in unknown or unforeseen ways by the agents of multinational commerce. There are also problems generated by the diversity of cultures and varieties of individual values and needs, which are compounded by differing ideologies and stages of economic development across the world. These complexities are compounded again by the fact that the decisions to be made are frequently those of policy or strategy. That is, they will direct broad arrays of activity over considerable periods of time and structure responses to as yet unforeseen events and opportunities. Discerning the preferences and difficulties of relevantly affected people, in other words, will be difficult.

BASIC AND SECONDARY WANTS

With several simple and plausible assumptions in hand, however, the difficulties which beset utilitarian approaches can be addressed. The great majority of people, whatever their circumstances, have very strong interests in life and the means required to sustain it. However diverse their lives, prospects, ideologies or cultures, it is plausible to assume individuals will place great weight on maintaining these. It is also plausible to assume that agents who imperil human life and the means to sustain it have done great harm. Seeking to provide the greatest good for the greatest number of people, therefore, amounts to a fundamental obligation to preserve human life and its means, on the assumption that 'human good' is ultimately defined by what humans prefer. These fundamental and universal desires for life and the means to sustain it can be termed 'basic wants'. If human beings have any obligations at all to one another, the duty to preserve human life and the requirements for life must be primary, given the assumption that this is what people most fundamentally desire. In normal circumstances, therefore, this obligation to preserve human life and the means to sustain it will be the most fundamental obligation human beings have to others, carrying more weight than other specific duties they may come to possess.

This fundamental obligation has several notable features. For one, it is usually neither difficult nor enormously expensive to meet its requirements. A diet sufficient for normal human activity, as well as shelter, clothing and basic medical care are not costly; they are cheap. Sustaining the entire world is well within the means of advanced industrialized nations. An effort of this sort certainly would not dwarf other expenses governments willingly shoulder, such as maintaining military forces or retirement programs.[14] The material costs, in other words, are both finite and comparatively modest. Second, these requirements will occasionally generate conflict. This may occur when the basic requirements of some persons conflict with those of others, or when basic requirements conflict with other tastes and aspirations humans possess. As elaborated shortly, basic requirements of human life should be weighed only against other basic requirements and not bartered against the lesser concerns of human beings.

Lastly, it is a truism that human individuals or other moral agents can only be morally obliged to do what they are able. This implies that no single human being or human institution can be obligated to maintain everyone in the world. Individuals and institutions can, however, be expected to avoid depriving others of the requirements for life and expected, as well, to endeavor to supply the requirements of life to all. The limitations of human nature are also relevant here. Humans are limited not only in their command of material resources but in knowledge, energy, time and emotional attachments. This finitude sets bounds on what individuals are able to accomplish. This is not an argument for complacency, however. Acknowledging these limitations removes one excuse for quiescence. It is commonly claimed that, because the problem of providing the resources of life for all cannot be solved, it is just as well to do nothing. But a response of some sort, even if it is inadequate, is better than nothing. Among the incessant themes of this work is that both persons and institutions are capable of doing much more than they previously have been to provide the basic requirements of life for others, but it both acknowledges that there are limits and seeks to disclose what can be accomplished within these constraints.

In well-ordered societies, however, people are apt to give little thought to the basic requirements of life. Their lives will be focused on other pursuits, and this is as it should be. They come to seek flavor and variety in food, rather than simple nourishment. They want clothes and shelter which are stylish or luxurious rather than minimally adequate. And they seek rewarding endeavor in the sciences, arts or commerce over and above the bare struggle to remain alive. Notice, however, that these interests vary widely from person to person and place to place, and that they are vastly more costly and difficult to supply than the basic requirements of life.

These interests are thus at the mercy of whim and fashion. They are not fixed and stable in the manner of basic wants. While basic wants can be served cheaply, there is no limit to the expense required to serve the desires generated by ever-inventive human imagination. Elemental food and shelter, for example, are cheap, but there is little upper limit to the expense of lavish mansions or extravagant clothing. Serving these desires must be vastly more costly and difficult than providing for primary wants. Futhermore, meeting them will often demand far greater intrusion into people's lives than merely providing food and shelter. Satisfying careers, rich cultural life or elevated standards of living require certain types of social structure, which can only be established at the cost of changing the way people live.

Furthermore, though people spend much of their time and energy in pursuit of these lesser wants, when push comes to shove they are highly likely to give greatest weight to the basic requirements for life. These lesser desires can, therefore, be termed 'secondary wants'. Secondary wants must be parasitic on those which are basic, because they cannot be enjoyed unless life itself is present. These secondary wants, therefore, are of much less importance than the basic requirements, and the obligation people have to supply them for others is correspondingly less, and also more apt to be overridden by other considerations. Their moral importance is further undermined by the practical difficulties: namely, that they are more varied, vastly more costly, more difficult to satisfy and in some instances require more intrusive means for their satisfaction.[15]

Individual human beings, therefore, always have a strong obligation to seek to maintain the basic requirements of all persons wherever they are found, subject to the limitations of human nature and human circumstance. They have much weaker obligations – as a general rule – to endeavor to satisfy secondary wants. In fact, this obligation will sometimes be completely swept aside by other concerns.

There is a complication: people take on special obligations by various means. Among these are personal obligations, as of parents to children; professional obligations, as with the particular responsibilities of physicians, government officials or police officers; and institutional obligations (those which people acquire when they join human institutions). In fact, people frequently devote more of their attention and energy to serving these specific obligations than the more general and basic ones.

The perspective of this work allows a ready justification of these obligations. Special obligations are morally justified if they are important instruments for meeting the basic or the secondary wants of human beings. If they fail to do so, such obligations are morally neutral at best. They gain whatever legitimacy they possess only by reference to human aspiration, even if the chain of connection is lengthy and convoluted. This implies, further, that these obligations cannot outweigh or overrule those that are more fundamental. Special obligations cannot outweigh the obligation to provide the basic requirements of life for human beings *unless* these obligations are necessary to support an institution which is better suited to meet these requirements, or does so on a larger scale.

THE OBLIGATIONS OF CORPORATIONS AND OF PEOPLE WITHIN THEM

For the present work, the implications of the above position are clear. Individual human beings always retain the fundamental obligation to provide for the basic wants of others. This remains true when they function as members of an institution, with special obligations resulting from this association. Where there is conflict, the obligation to preserve human life must always take precedence over special obligations. Often though, corporations will play important roles in providing the means of human life. This, too, must be taken into account. However, humans and the institutions they create do not have as strong an obligation to meet secondary wants for others. Indeed, there are often good practical reasons, mentioned earlier, why they should refrain from explicit attempts to do so. Furthermore, most institutions serve these needs in one fashion or another. Hence, people have reason to assume, as a rule of thumb, that their activities within organizations will play some constructive role in meeting secondary wants. Sometimes, of course, there will be direct conflict between the interests and actions of an institution and the secondary wants of people. When this occurs, responsible persons within institutions must confront the moral quandary. The direction of resolution suggested in this work is that they have the obligation to weigh the overall contribution to human good provided by the institution's function against the palpable harm done in this case, and ask whether the harm done is necessary either for the institution's functioning or for its survival.[16] These deliberations will be neither simple nor precise, but there will be cases, as with some celebrated instances of whistleblowing, when the moral obligations of persons will require that they step outside their institutional role and override the special responsibilities they have within it.

The above is directed at individual persons; it is also necessary to examine the moral standards which properly apply to whole institutions (in this instance, corporate enterprises).

The prospect of corporations becoming deeply involved in moral crusading is distinctly unsettling. Their wealth, resources and control over their employees give them considerable influence, which can be used as powerfully for evil as for good. Since corporations are closely controlled by small segments of society, their influence can easily be directed to parochial concerns. Since they are private, they are not accountable to the larger public in the way a governmental agency might be. Few would regard the prospect of forceful corporate entry into the debates over abortion, pornography or foreign assistance with equanimity. Where they have entered the lists in such matters, as where oil companies with extensive interests in the Middle East have become involved in the foreign policy of their home nations, their activities are commonly distinctly self-interested, and lack credibility as the result.[17]

Those instances where corporations have worked for social change do not inspire confidence either. They have been willing to cultivate dictators or rogue colonels in hopes of creating a profitable environment for themselves. The effort of International Telephone and Telegraph to remove President Allende of Chile and replace him with a more amenable figure stands out as the paradigm of a clumsy effort at engineering change which was also blatantly self-interested.[18]

In the light of the above, few would seek to involve corporations in attempts to mold human life to accord with corporate ideals, and few would look with complacency on the efforts of a small minority of powerful individuals to wield influence in the service of their own moral predilections. There is much to be said for restricting corporate activity to tending business concerns and leaving moral issues to institutions explicitly designed to respond to them. After all, the common complaint is that corporations are overly powerful and overly adept at getting their way in the world. If their endeavors extend to explicitly moral and social matters, their influence may become even more pervasive and their power more menacing.

The above has considerable force. In fact, if it were possible to choose between corporations having moral concerns and avoiding them, the latter would be the obvious choice. The difficulty is that this option is not available. The size, power and reach of corporations, which makes their presence so fearful, also guarantees that their actions will have significant effects on the lives and well-being of large numbers of people. These consequences entail that corporations are inescapably involved in issues of moral import. The question, therefore, cannot be whether they should become involved but how and to what extent.

The sketch of these concerns also, however, reveals the shape of an answer. There is an important difference between working to do good (that is, seeking to improve the world) and seeking only to avoid doing harm or merely to repair harm one has caused. There are persuasive reasons for believing that corporations should not undertake to do good or to improve the world. This effort would require that corporations use their resources and influence to mold the world to their liking. Because they are private, because they are controlled by only a few people, and because they are designed to promote commerce, they are likely to be both dangerous and inept if they seek to shape the world to suit themselves.

In addition, whatever good corporations achieve in the world results from their talent for commercial endeavor. They contribute to human well-being by creating jobs, providing goods and services, and efficiently managing resources. Insofar as they also become involved in moral crusading, they will become less adept at providing these. Furthermore, different corporations would very probably enlist in opposing crusades, which would likely breed conflict resulting in economic chaos, and leave the world worse than under present arrangements.

Structure of Response 33

In some ways corporations resemble military forces, which also command great power, are under the control of a few, and are designed to serve narrowly defined purposes. When military leaders are moved to shape the world in accordance with their own vision, as they sometimes are, the results are generally disastrous.

Corporations and military forces are quite different from governments. Even closely controlled governments are sensitive to a broad array of influences and are designed to cope with large social issues. This does not imply that governments are always benign or adept in their function. It is only that governments are better suited to respond to social problems and improve the conditions of human life than are military forces or business enterprises. Governments, in other words, and not corporations should take the initiative in addressing social ills and improving human life.

Many issues, therefore, should not be left to corporate initiative but are more appropriately matters for public debate and regulation. Matters of affirmative action or quotas on hiring fall into this category. These are questions of public regulation and should be decided through the resources of public institutions rather than the decisions of private institutions. This does not imply that corporations should fail to initiate steps to address problems once social priorities have been established by public means. They should be more than inert bystanders when public policy addresses concerns which directly involve them, such as those of discrimination in employment or environmental pollution. Of course, corporations face particular difficulties when public policy appears immoral or misguided. Addressing these problems is part of the labor of the following chapters.

Corporations must, in addition, hold themselves accountable for the harm which their activities cause for individual human beings. Managers are able to direct corporate operations and redirect corporate activity to meet new circumstances or remedy the effects of past conduct. Corporations, as claimed in an earlier chapter, are moral agents and therefore have the responsiblities that constrain other sorts of moral agents. Though seeking only to avoid harm and working to achieve positive benefit often intertwine, these two goals are separated by clear differences in scope and emphasis. Corporations are responsible for harmful consequences which result from their own operations. Simply to conduct their affairs intelligently, corporations must have sophisticated information about conditions in nations where they operate, and be able to make projections about future developments, as well as to estimate the array of consequences of engaging in one set of ventures rather than another.[19] They already, in other words, have the substantive basis for making decisions about the consequences of their conduct for people's lives. All that remains is for them explicitly to ask the right questions and involve themselves seriously in the quest to avoid harm to others.

In sum, corporations and those functioning within them have the strong obligation to avoid actions and policies which are likely to deprive people of their lives or means to life. This obligation must generally have greater moral weight than the survival of the corporation itself. However, as claimed in Chapter 1, it is rare that corporations will be faced with this choice and, when they are, it will be obvious that the choice entails anguished moral difficulty.

Corporations and their employees will have much weaker obligations to serve the secondary wants of human beings. This is both because these wants are morally less weighty and because of the practical difficulties and unbounded costs, mentioned earlier, in the way of meeting them. Furthermore, the intrusion into human and cultural life necessary to begin to meet them will be inappropriate for corporations.

It appears that Milton Friedman was not far from being correct.[20] In terms of the language of this chapter, he claimed that the special responsibilities of people within corporations and the corporate obligations of honesty and fairness when dealing with others are all that matter. He was correct in believing this is a substantial portion of corporate obligation, whether of employees or of corporations as a whole. He, and others, were also correct in believing that corporations should avoid social engineering or moral crusading.[21] He was mistaken, however, in believing that these are the only areas of moral concern. The fundamental argument of this work is that the sense of corporate moral accountability, whose existence is acknowledged even by staunch free-marketeers such as Friedman himself, must be expanded in one way. Corporations and their employees must take account of, and accept responsibility for, the consequences for preserving and maintaining human life which result from corporate activity.

Though this expansion of accountability and sensitivity seems simple and straightforward, trivial perhaps, its consequences are far-reaching. The following chapters are devoted to examining the major areas in which these difficulties are likely to be encountered in the arena of multinational commerce.

3 Corporate Size and Power

It is neither conceptually nor empirically necessary that multinational corporations be huge or enormously wealthy. Numerous middling and small enterprises are happily and profitably engaged in multinational commerce. Moreover, as the global economy becomes more tightly integrated and homogeneous, business enterprises of all sizes and configurations will seek opportunity in the world market.

Nonetheless, several features of the international arena favor giant commercial operations. Only large enterprises are likely to have the resources to scatter portions of their corporate organism across the globe. A crucial factor, mentioned earlier, is that there are presently single global markets for many products, and corporate leaders have discovered that they must be active in all segments of each if they are to compete successfully. This necessity is the result of several factors. Abandoning the bulk of the world's markets to competitors will concede to them the advantage of greater resources, more numerous ties with governments and other enterprises, and the prospect of economies of scale, as well as more options for profitable endeavor. For the same reasons, all corporations, in order to remain viable, are driven to seek continued growth and, to a far greater degree than in past years, the arena of this growth is the global market.[1]

Also, multinational commerce allows corporations to expand beyond whatever natural bounds are fixed when their operations are confined to the domain of a single nation-state. Arcing across national boundaries allows them to employ more people, control more resources, manipulate more markets or swallow up more subsidiaries than they otherwise might.[2]

These trends are exacerbated by the facility with which multinational corporations concoct joint ventures and cooperate in other ways which decrease competitive strife but increase the scope and intensity of corporate influence. The great size and influence of individual enterprises is therefore multiplied by joining forces with others.[3]

THE DANGERS OF CORPORATE LEVIATHANS

Huge corporations pose difficulty for all governments and all people, but their greatest threat is to poor, small, underdeveloped nations with few resources and little expertise of the sort required to joust with vast enterprises.[4] The problems and hazards result from the sheer bulk of their operations, the influence which their resources allow and their ability to dominate legal systems or evade effective legal control.

Mammoth corporations tend to conceptualize in terms of billions of dollars and devise projects which create huge factories or sprawling networks of plantations. For smaller, less developed nations (those lacking an existing base of industrial plants, skilled managers or governmental leaders with the expertise and resources to cope with such vastness), huge commercial projects can result in substantial disruption. The land required for ambitious developments may displace peasants from their holdings, but leave no place for them to go and provide no opportunity for work. The projects themselves may devour sufficient resources and manpower that the whole economy of a nation is distorted. This can be disastrous. The resources of a small nation can be so thoroughly absorbed by vast projects that few remain to produce the goods necessary to sustain the lives of peasants or urban laborers. This problem is particularly acute for agri-business concerns which can engulf the agricultural capacity of a country such that its population can be fed only by importing food. Also, national production can easily become geared to a single product, which means that a sharp drop in world demand can result in economic hardship for the entire nation.

In addition, the sheer size and resources of these corporations gives them the ability to exert substantial influence. In past years, they were commonly able to gain aggressive support from the governments of their home nations when they became embroiled in adversity with host nations. At present, governments no longer dispatch troops abroad to protect corporate investment, but they are frequently willing to underwrite the efforts of native corporations in more subtle ways.[5] Furthermore, the ruling groups of would-be host nations are commonly anxious to secure their presence and often likely to profit from their activity. As a result, they may be anxious to facilitate investment by whatever means are available and willing to take measures to ensure that no local groups, whether unions or political activists, disrupt corporate endeavor. Corporations in these circumstances can easily, perhaps effortlessly, shape local conditions to allow comfortable operation and may do so without pausing to consider the effects of their activity on the local economic and social environment. The assets of multinational corporations may also strain the resources of national governments in legal matters. The legal tangle resulting from the disastrous leak of toxic gas at the Union Carbide plant in Bhopal, India, in 1984 provides an excellent illustration of this problem. More than 2500 people died as a result of the incident and over 200000 others were injured.[6] The government of India brought a suit against Union Carbide on behalf of some 500000 claimants. The battle was fought in courts in India and the United States for over four years. It was settled without coming to trial in 1989 when the Indian Supreme Court accepted an arrangement by which the company agreed to pay $470 million to the victims and their families.[7]

Ironies abound in this case, but several are especially pertinent. One is that the government of India, the plaintiff in the case (because it undertook to represent those who had filed claims), initially sought to bring the case to court in the United States rather than in its own legal system. In part, this was because the government wanted to make sure that the parent company, rather than its Indian subsidiary, would be reached by the case and that it would be held accountable for the actions of its subsidiary. But another part of the motivation of the Union of India is thought to be due to the fact that it is commonly agreed that US courts grant higher monetary damages than anywhere else in the world and because US legal rules of evidence regarding liability are easier for plaintiffs to meet than elsewhere.[8] A second irony is that the plaintiff's own statutes governing hazardous substances were less strict and detailed than in the US, and part of the controversy of the case was that Union Carbide was functioning under looser standards in India than it might have elsewhere.[9]

In the legal tangle following Bhopal, additionally, more than simply the courts were stretched to their limit and perhaps beyond.[10] The Indian government was hard pressed to match the legal resources which Union Carbide was able to marshal for the suit. The thought that an equivalent accident could occur elsewhere, in a nation lacking the resources and legal traditions of India, is sobering indeed.

Where legal resources are unequally distributed, or where courts and statutes are inadequate to meet the complex requirements of huge enterprises and of contemporary technology, legal maneuvering will be dominated by those groups that enjoy a monopoly of wealth, expertise and experience, or it is possible that the activities of huge enterprises may fail to be subject to adequate legal regulation.

Immense and aggressive multinational corporations are thus apt to cause difficulties of three sorts for host nations. These difficulties are *morally* important because they have significant consequences for the lives and welfare of great numbers of people. The scale and complexity of their operations may disrupt or distort a nation's economy in ways that will make it more vulnerable to economic upset or will complicate the efforts of citizens to gain a decent livelihood. Next, corporate intruders may use their resources to sway dominant groups in order to achieve corporate goals or enlist home governments to support their efforts. Once again, these efforts may warp local economies or endanger the livelihood of ordinary citizens. Lastly, the legal structure of a nation may be inadequate to cope with the issues that accompany the intrusion of of a large and sophisticated corporation. Moreover, the legal resources of such enterprises may enable them to dominate whatever legal undertakings occur. As the Bhopal incident and the efforts of victims and their families to gain compensation illustrate, the consequences of these legal issues for the lives of ordinary people can be great indeed.

THE BENEFITS OF MULTINATIONALS

The above matters are grave and important. Nonetheless, a balanced picture, as well as a deeper understanding of the issues, demands recognition that the presence of huge multinational corporations in nations can have significant benefits. Several of the nations that railed against the activities of multinational corporations a few years ago, or forced them to withdraw altogether, are now actively courting their interest.[11] This transformation is the result of multiple factors. First, corporations can be a source of badly needed capital for investment and economic progress. Schemes for national development commonly require large infusions of capital and ambitious projects. They are, in other words, the very sort of endeavors which enormous multinational corporations are well suited to undertake.

Economic development, moreover, is commonly believed to require advanced technology and sophisticated management techniques, resources readily found within the domain of the major multinational corporations. It is no accident that China and the USSR, which a short time ago were bastions of the struggle against capitalism, are now ardently seeking the interest of foreign private enterprise to assist their economic rebuilding. Another factor which enhances the importance of corporate investment is that, in recent years, assistance from governments of wealthy nations has remained constant while the need for capital by underdeveloped nations has increased. This is exacerbated by the debt crisis of recent years, which has made international banks wary of granting additional loans to struggling economies. To meet their needs, developing nations have therefore been forced to place increased reliance on multinational corporations as private sources of finance. Furthermore, the devices nations have developed to attempt to cope with the debt crisis, such as debt-equity swaps, depend for their success on greater participation by international corporations.[12]

'Development', moreover, has come to be understood as the effort to create industrialized economies, based on technological sophistication, which are modelled after those of the wealthiest and most powerful nations of the world. There seems no fundamental reason why all nations should formulate their economic goals in this way, other than the understandable wish to emulate success and the desire to gain the power which accompanies this success. With this perspective, however, joining the world economy becomes necessary.

Entering the world economy may also have become necessary in the more basic sense mentioned earlier of simply preserving a minimal standard of life for all citizens. However, note that this standard, measured in terms of medical care, life expectancy, education, income levels and nutrition, is also derived from the paradigm set by advanced industrialized nations. The 'minimum' of the latter portion of this century certainly differs from the 'minimum' of a century or two ago. Furthermore, governments of nation-states are held more tightly to account for preserving this minimum than in past years, adding further pressure to follow the Western model of development. Even totalitarian governments are wont ostentatiously to announce the goals of meeting the material needs of their citizens and improving their prospects of life. This is vividly illustrated by Iran. Since the fall of the Shah in 1979, it has been caught in intense and austere religious fervor. Nonetheless, its leaders have recently found themselves under considerable pressure to improve the economic welfare of the Iranian people and have been forced to restrain their program of Islamic revolution in order to do so.[13]

Another difficulty which developing nations face is the result of their ability to create modern educational systems or dispatch young people abroad for advanced training before they can offer careers which utilize the educated people they produce. The social unrest of several nations results in part from the fact that they have large pools of young people with advanced degrees but no jobs to make use of their education. Multinational corporations can be important sources of positions which employ the skilled laborers as well as the managerial and professional personnel of host nations. This has not always been the case. In the past many companies preferred to import managerial and professional employees from their home nations, but it was neither necessary nor inevitable that these policies continue. Nations that are adept at coping with corporate leviathans have devised statutes and crafted agreements which demand significant training and employment of local workers for positions which are other than menial.[14]

A balanced discussion also requires acknowledging that multinational corporations are not necessarily more harmful or self-seeking than strictly domestic enterprises. In fact, some assert that the latter can be more manipulative and less responsible within their home nation-state than more cosmopolitan firms.[15] What is more, their influence may be more invidious and less susceptible to public influence than multinational corporations, which have greater visibility. In fact, some of the vituperation directed at multinational concerns has come from domestic enterprises seeking to protect their own perquisites.

Some of the controversy which envelops multinational corporations, in other words, may simply be the normal friction between business enterprises and governments that occurs in the course of day-to-day relations. When foreign intruders are present, the difficulties may be magnified and the friction more intense just because they are foreign. Further, their alien status frequently makes multinational corporations convenient targets of national frustration, which may be manipulated by politicians seeking to distract attention from other issues.[16] Bear in mind also that politically and economically dominant groups often enjoy close ties, particularly in developing nations. Intimacy of this sort can prevent the overt friction and hostility which may arise when less closely connected groups deal with one another.

PRESENT CONDITIONS

As the above illustrates, large and influential multinational corporations are potent influences, but their influence can be good or ill, or a mixture of both. All depends on the manner and context in which they function. However, because it happens that most nations of the world look to the advanced industrialized nations as paradigms of their goal for development and that participation in international commerce appears necessary to sustain material well-being or promote economic development, the nations of the world are fated to deal with multinational corporations and must learn to come to terms with them. In recent years, moreover, most nations appear to have decided that, on balance, the benefit to be gained from hosting their activities outweighs the considerable difficulties.

Furthermore, the picture of responsibility for difficulties related to corporate size and power is complex, and has evolved over time. The problems of a few decades ago arose not simply because of corporate size and power but also because underdeveloped host nations lacked the experience and expertise to cope effectively with their presence and because there were few international institutions, standards and practices designed to oversee multinational commerce. The swift rush of corporations into transnational commerce, combined with the concurrent and equally sudden emergence of newly independent, but underdeveloped and inexperienced nations in the period following the Second World War, created a situation in which abuses, mistakes and oversights were inevitable. This was exacerbated by the mixture of vulnerablilty felt by new nations, and the seeming invincibility and total dominance of Western European nations and their corporate emissaries during that era.[17]

The conditions of the immediate post-war era, in other words, provided fertile breeding grounds for corporate arrogance and self-assurance, while developing nations believed themselves powerless to resist corporate attentions and felt constrained to accommodate them. Of course, there are exceptions to this picture. American corporations have been active in Latin America since the last century. While their self-assurance long remained undiminished, the sense of weakness their presence generated in Latin American nations has long since bred a countervailing nationalism, resulting in protracted strife. Nonetheless, the central fact is that these factors have largely changed in recent decades. Multinational corporations are no longer blithely self-assured and no longer aggressively supported by their home governments. The embattled nationalism of new nations, along with their accumulated experience and growing self-assurance, has provided them with effective tools for coping with corporate guests. The dangers of corporate size and power remain, but in a different form from past years. Corporations presently seeking entry to a nation play a much more passive role than in the past.

Decisions about programs of economic development, and the corporate role within them, are now made by others. At present, those with greatest influence include the governing elites of host nations and the major international financial institutions, such as the IMF and the World Bank. While the governments of the great economic powers can do a great deal to shape the climate of world trade, their present levels of financial assistance preclude a more direct role in developing nations. They retain indirect influence via their positions in the IMF, World Bank and the GATT, and can shape the policies of development adopted by these groups. The international debt crisis has sapped the interest transnational banks once had in developing nations, leaving the quasi-public financial institutions and the elites of developing nations as the principal agents.

There is presently a consensus that multinational corporations have a central role to play in schemes of national economic development, but there is disagreement and uncertainty concerning what these plans, and the corporate role in them, should be. While the world has gained considerable experience in these matters in the past decades, and there is perhaps greater realism and mutual understanding on all sides, much perplexity remains. The extent of this confusion is vividly illustrated by recurrent claims that the conditions stipulated by the IMF as requirements for receiving loans are ineffectual, and perhaps counterproductive.

Corporations are not well suited to devising plans of national economic development. But the reason for this is not that they are unable to devise intelligent and enlightened programs of development or tailor them to the specific circumstances of particular nation-states; they could do so easily, and perhaps with greater alacrity than nations themselves. In fact, there is at least one case, that of Argentina, where corporate planners have been retained to perform this function.[18]

Rather, the difficulties are practical. A very basic practical requirement is that each nation must have a single cohesive program of development in which every corporate actor has its assigned role. It is also practically necessary that a single agency monitor and direct this process and be accountable for its outcome. Solitary corporate operators are not well situated to perform these offices, and disaster would result if each corporation active in a nation veered off on its own plan of development.

Furthermore, and most importantly, because there is protracted debate in governmental, scholarly and financial circles on the topic of which strategies of development are best and most effective, it is best that those most closely connected with host nations make decisions on contentious issues of economic planning. Governing elites are frequently self-serving, but they are more likely to share the fate of poor choices than alien multinational corporations. These are matters about which there may be honest and informed differences of opinion. Where perplexity of this magnitude exists, corporations are ill-advised to intrude with their own opinions. This examination reinforces the conclusion of earlier discussions. Corporations should not undertake projects which are designed to make the world a better or more humane place. Neither should they attempt to mold the world in their own image or shape it to their own ideals. Their role in the economic and technological progress of nations has become, and should remain, essentially that of passive collaborators with national governments.

Nevertheless, this does not imply that multinational corporations are entirely free of moral responsibility for the ways in which their projects shape the welfare of human beings. It is reasonable to expect corporations to acknowledge responsibility for avoiding schemes which will result in significant and obvious harm for the people of a nation. Though the choice of strategies for economic development remains steeped in controversy, there will be cases where particular programs will clearly result in great harm to individual persons or to a nation as a whole, and corporations have the responsibility to avoid *these*. It is not unreasonable to expect them to do this. The information and feel for local conditions they routinely acquire before making investment decisions also enables them to foresee outcomes of this sort. A number of corporations take these problems seriously and have adopted policies designed to avoid them.[19] This result is obviously consistent with the general position of this work. Corporations do not have the responsibility to seek to improve the world or enrich and enlighten the nations where they conduct business. Corporations can, however, be expected to avoid causing harm.

The institutions best situated to develop wise strategies of economic development and ensure that foreign corporate presence is beneficial rather than harmful are the governments of nation-states. In addition, no schemes of development can hope to be effective without the endorsement and vigorous cooperation of sovereign governments. Given the present condition of the world, they, not corporations, must be the principal agents overseeing these matters.

It remains true that national governments are sometimes obstacles to wise policies of development. Their policies may be shortsighted, inept, repressive or crafted to benefit a small dominant elite. So long as nations cling successfully to the perquisites of sovereign authority, however, there are few means to remedy these problems forcefully.

Meliorist responses, in other words, may sometimes be all that are available. This will be particularly true where, as is presently the case, there is a substantial disagreement and uncertainty in the international community on matters concerning the most promising strategies for development or the proper role which multinational corporations should play within them.

Where none has the clear authority, power or wisdom to force wise choices on nations, meliorist responses of providing information and expert assistance, or making optimal use of influential agencies, are all that are available. These responses cannot suffice to ensure universal acceptance of wise policies or even to ensure that the activities of all the powerful groups which shape the economy of a nation are coordinated with one another. However, the good offices made available by these responses can be used by nations genuinely seeking to improve the lot of their citizens.

In addition world opinion and influential financial institutions can exert at least some pressure on recalcitrant governments. This is not an ideal solution, but it is better than nothing and may result in considerable good. Several measures are available to the institutions guiding international commerce and finance which can begin to address problems of skewed development. Financial institutions, including the World Bank and the IMF, are among the major sources of development capital for developing nations. The World Bank is the single largest source of their funds. It is important for these institutions to redirect their policies to meet issues of development and the role of multinational corporations in such developments more directly and with greater open-mindedness. Their approach in the past has tended to be fiscally and politically conservative and to overlook issues of this sort.[20] The United Nations is another center with a major role to play. The difficulty is that its operations are often heavily influenced by representatives of the same governmental elites whose agenda is frequently part of the problem. Nevertheless, UN bureaucrats have examined these issues carefully and have worked to formulate prudent guidelines for economic aspiration.[21] Finally, the great economic and political powers – the members of the Group of Seven, for example – could, if they put their collective minds to it, devise guidelines to govern investment and manufacturing by multinational corporations.[22] Indeed, there are some problems, including the current international debt crisis, that can be effectively managed only through the attentions of the great economic powers. Corporations, whether singly or collectively, are simply not capable of addressing these issues in forceful fashion, and neither would it be wise for them to do so. The principal agents of response must be located in other institutions. Once again, the approach to these issues must be meliorist. It must be meliorist because no clear answers to questions of development are available, such answers as are devised cannot be implemented with precision or authority, *and* there will be new and unexpected crises which can only be addressed in the same haphazard and uncoordinated fashion as before. It is likely, however, that as the world becomes more fully integrated economically and crises of international commerce continue to emerge, the international community will gradually become more adept at coping with them. National governments will necessarily play a central role in all of this. In years to come, moreover, it is possible that the most significant role governments play will gradually shift to that of international facilitators and coordinators of commerce, rather than as wielders of military and political power. It may be, in other words, that the role and status of national governments will come to merge gradually with that foreseen for international bureaucracies.

The problems arising from disparity of legal resources must also be resolved incrementally over time. The beginning of an adequate response to the problem of legal control of multinational corporations and inequality of legal resources must contain several elements. Corporations generally appear willing to be governed by the laws of the nations where they function.[23] Of course, they can be expected to press their advantage within these legal structures as far as possible. They will continue to be aggressive and self-interested, but they can be adequately controlled, provided the necessary legal structures are in place. The Bhopal case vividly illustrates the point that it is sometimes necessary for human welfare that this legal machinery exist. India was fortunate to have an existing legal structure which could serve as the foundation of an instrument of effective control. As the Indian government itself has insisted, much needs to be done to effect this transformation. Other developing nations may have far fewer legal resources to cope with the demands of contemporary corporate endeavor.

It is apparent that international efforts and international cooperation are necessary to meet these requirements. Among India's needs is a set of statutes governing corporate activity, as well as the control of hazardous substances, advanced technology and the transport of finished goods. These requirements could be met simply through a set of model statutes, which could be modified as individual nations wished. The United Nations is well suited for an undertaking of this sort.

A need more difficult to supply is for courts, and the personnel to operate them, which will be capable of handling the complex and difficult cases that may arise when multinational corporations are present. The problem is exacerbated by the limited resources of many developing nations and by the fact that such cases are apt to be fairly rare in nations without widespread economic development. Without a developed body of legal cases, the human experience and legal structures equipped to deal with them are unlikely to evolve. Courts and lawyers in India, for example, were inexperienced in gathering and safeguarding evidence. They lacked teams of people with the resources to manage such cases. They lacked courtroom proceedures designed to manage them efficiently. As before, it appears that international bodies are best suited to address these needs. It is possible that the most adequate solution would be to establish an international pool of legal expertise and of specialists in various sorts of litigation, as well as teams of people adept in the various chores of collecting evidence, interviewing witnesses or managing the day-to-day details of a long and complex court proceeding. These resources could be made available by agencies of the United Nations to nations in need of them, as it has already done in related areas.[24] This effort would go a long way toward helping nations compete on equal terms with large corporations.

It may also be necessary to devise unusual legal instruments for meeting the special needs of those in developing nations. In the Bhopal case, for instance, the government of India undertook to represent the claimants. It is very likely that this was necessary to ensure that the impoverished, uneducated and powerless individuals received adequate representation. It is entirely possible that further experience with cases of this sort will reveal other needs that must be met in an equally creative fashion.

Along with the above efforts, it is necessary to refine international law to met the emerging demands of multinational commerce, which continues to grow exponentially. One important result of the Bhopal case is that it clearly established the legal principle that the parent corporations of multinational enterprises will be held accountable for the failings of their subsidiaries.[25] Among the problems posed by sprawling multinational concerns is the difficulty of establishing clear lines of responsibility and authority for the conduct of the total entity. It is necessary that a body of international law be refined to clarify these matters. It would also be valuable to have internationally accepted standards of evidence and liability, so that both nations and corporations have a clear understanding of what their legal obligations are and are clearly aware of the nature and intricacies of legal procedure.

The multinational corporations are certainly not able to create these changes. The motivation must come from the international community and from individual governments. At present there will frequently be cases where the legal responsibilities of corporations are unclear or where there is no existing body of law to regulate their activities. Hence there will be many areas where corporations have no clearly defined legal responsibilities. This does *not* imply that they will lack moral accountability. They retain the fundamental moral responsibility to avoid action which harms or endangers human life or the means of life. Where corporate legal obligations are unclear and moral standards are fragmentary or matters of controversy, it will sometimes be difficult to discern exactly what responsibilities corporations possess. Nonetheless, there will sometimes be obvious cases of activities which corporations should avoid and others where they will be required simply to exercise good judgment and good-will.

At present, the circumstances of world commerce indicate that large and powerful multinational corporations will continue to dominate international commerce, and that developing nations will continue to seek such corporations' presence as a means of furthering their own economic welfare. In coming years there are likely to be greater numbers of large corporations in developing nations, and the scope and intensity of their activity will increase. Hence the problems associated with corporate size and power must be met on an ever larger scale, even as corporations, governments and international bodies become more adept at managing them. The lesson of this chapter is that national governments and international bodies must be the major agents for coping with these matters, particularly in issues of economic development and systems of legal control. Corporations themselves will remain essentially passive participants in these efforts, although they retain the moral obligation to avoid activities that endanger human life and well-being.

4 Cultural and Economic Diversity

The wide ranging activity of multinational corporations brings them in touch with great differences in culture and economic standards in various parts of the world. They may encounter patterns of conduct, or standards of the treatment of human beings or preservation of the ecosystem which are markedly different from corporate policies in effect elsewhere. When such conditions prevail, corporations will find themselves faced with the dilemma of wishing to uphold standards which they normally accept elsewhere, yet constrained to conform to the standards of practice in the locale where they operate. This pressure may be intensified by their desire to avoid cultural and moral imperialism or the need to hew to local practice in order to continue doing business.

Their conflict cannot be resolved by adopting the straightforward policy of obeying national laws where they function. Quite obviously, keeping to local statute must be a general rule of corporate practice.[1] This policy cannot be the final answer, however, because cases will arise which it cannot accommodate. In some instances cultural practices will not be explicitly encapsulated within law or may be clearly outside the law, yet may effectively shape ways of doing business. Also, it is possible that national laws may require corporations to perform actions which are clearly morally impermissible according to their own standards, such as laws requiring them to inform governments of the activities of political dissidents or those requiring them to offer only menial positions to members of particular ethnic groups or social classes.

CULTURAL AND IDEOLOGICAL DIFFERENCES

The difficulties multinational corporations are presently apt to encounter fall into several different categories. Among them is the great variety in local standards regulating the status of ethnic groups, races or the sexes throughout the world. In the United States or

Western Europe most corporations will, in official policy at least, confirm that women are the equals of men and should therefore have full access to all positions within an economy. Corporations may also be willing to practise affirmative action to help ensure that they do so. A rough consensus has been reached among the nations bordering the North Atlantic that treating women differently from men – segregating them or regarding them as incapable of performing certain roles within an economy – is both morally objectionable and rationally unsupportable. Yet there are cultures of the world (Islamic, for example) in which religious standards demand that women should be strictly segregated from men outside the home, though they are not necessarily barred from commerce.[2] Corporations with branches in these nations, such as Saudi Arabia, may find it difficult to function in accordance with their avowed principles while also respecting the perspective of local culture. Nonetheless, where corporations have officially committed themselves to policies of sexual equality, they must regard discrimination, even when deeply embedded in a culture, as mistaken. If they feel they must continue to accommodate culture in these matters, there must be some explicit rationale for doing so.

Several of these nations, moreover, have domestic women's movements pressing for a greater role in their societies. Saudi Arabia, Egypt and Pakistan, in particular, have active women's groups. Hence sexual discrimination is not uncontroversial even within the world of Islam.[3] This complexity is nicely illustrated by the instance of Pakistan. During the regime of the late General Zia, it moved to reintroduce traditional Islamic ideas governing the role of women, yet it presently has a woman, Benazir Bhutto, as Prime Minister. A different aspect of the problem is that there are nations, such as Japan or several of the Latin American states, that officially eschew discrimination against women. Nonetheless, traditional attitudes and practices remain so strong that it is very difficult to conduct business without coming to terms with *de facto* sexual inequality.[4]

Discrimination against women is only one facet of the culturally embedded discrimination found in various areas of the world, however. There remain outcast classes in both Japan and India.[5] Though discrimination against members of these groups is officially outlawed in both nations, actual practice retains the imprint of traditional ways. In Japan there are also various minority groups, the Korean in particular, who are regarded with suspicion and aversion by the larger society and are consequently kept segregated in most areas of life.[6]

The most overt and vicious discrimination is, of course, that embedded in the policies of apartheid in South Africa. The problems South Africa poses are sufficiently complex and difficult to merit extended examination in a separate chapter, Chapter 7. Moreover, racial discrimination remains in force in many parts of the world in less overt fashion than South Africa, yet retains a presence strong enough to shape and tinge day-to-day affairs. Even Brazil, for example, which is a racial melting pot and known for its easy racial harmony, retains subtle modes of differential treatment based solely on complexion.[7] Corporations seeking entry to these locales will have to come to terms with such practices in one fashion or another simply to conduct business. Failure to confront these matters explicitly will result in a simple mirroring of local practice, and thus place corporations at odds with their own announced policies.

In recent years the issue of bribery has also generated considerable difficulty and perplexity for corporations. In several nations, the system of bribery is so deeply entrenched and so widely practised that it is nearly impossible to engage in commercial activity without offering bribes. The problem is so endemic that some nations, such as Mexico and the Philippines, have found it nearly impossible to eliminate widespread bribery even after determined efforts to do so.[8] Corporations wishing to avoid these practices are faced with the difficult choice of being unable to conduct affairs in these nations or being forced to avoid these areas of opportunity altogether, with the consequence of leaving markets to their less fastidious competitors and at the risk of placing themselves at a competitive disadvantage as a result. The stakes are therefore substantial.

The difficulties with bribery open the way for consideration of another matter. Corporations increasingly find themselves conducting operations in nations with ideologies very different from those of the liberal democracies of Western Europe. They are scrambling for toeholds in the various Marxist nations of the world, as well as in those that have recently cast off Marxist regimes.[9] While a number of Marxist nations are becoming progressively more liberal, both politically and economically, several Islamic nations are greatly attracted by the rigid fundamentalism practised in Iran.[10] Corporations continue to seek opportunity in Islamic nations and are likely to find themselves subject to pressure from fundamentalist politics when they do so.

The difficulty these ideologies pose is not simply that they thoroughly reshape political structures, but they embody conceptions of the relation of the individual to the state, of individual rights (or the lack of them) and of the nature and function of the state which are entirely different from those of Western Europe. Furthermore, to the extent that corporations become more deeply involved in such nations, have larger investments in plant and capital, greater numbers of employees and suppliers, or increasingly come to depend on products or services from these nations to sustain their operations, it may be more difficult for them to resist ideological pressures or avoid becoming enrolled as their agents.[11] In the more severely fundamentalist Islamic nations, for example, the religious law of the *Sha'ria* is the fundamental law of the land, so corporations may find themselves called upon to enforce religious tenets in their daily transactions, their dealings with employees or their enforcement of agreements. They may find, too, that business decisions are constrained by religious principles at odds with those of commerce.[12]

Corporations active in Marxist nations may find themselves pressured to dismiss or punish employees who are deemed politically unreliable. It is also possible that they may find themselves called upon to cooperate in the surveillance of employees' personal lives and political activities. They may, in addition, find themselves compelled to participate in state-driven programs for the political indoctrination of employees and therefore aiding the transmission of ideologies very different from their own.[13]

They may also encounter complications of other sorts. Both Marxist and Islamic nations have been aggressive in exporting their ideology and supporting revolutionary movements abroad. Corporations may find themselves pressed to cooperate in various ways in these expansionist ideological ventures.[14] These topics will receive thorough examination in Chapter 6, which deals with political manipulation.

DIVERSE ECONOMIC CONDITIONS

In addition, multinational corporations face problems resulting from the diverse levels of economic development of the nations they enter. Reasonable standards of worker and environmental safety are patchy in some nations and nearly non-existent in others. Furthermore, the prevailing wage in several underdeveloped nations is barely adequate to sustain a laborer's family or provide children with sufficient resources to allow them the prospect of a productive adulthood. Wages below a certain level may literally make the difference between life and death (if not for the workers themselves, then for members of their families). Where wages are sufficiently low, they may sustain life but only at the cost of a reduced life span, increased susceptibility to disease, and inadequate resources to maintain an energetic and satisfying existence.

The problem of worker income must be taken seriously, because one of the fundamental claims of this work is that all have the obligation to preserve human life and its means to the extent that they are able. However, corporate managers pondering this difficulty will also be pulled by other considerations. They may have chosen to enter a nation because its wage rates are low, and feel compelled to keep them as low as is feasible. This results from their responsibility, owed to shareholders and other members of the enterprise, to maximize profit, and also from their need to sustain the competitive posture of the enterprise. In addition, they may plausibly avow that they have done nothing to bring about the poverty of their host nation, are in fact assisting its development by their presence, and are therefore not obligated to do anything further.

A problem of distributive justice also lurks here. Other laborers may wonder why *they* do not receive the same wage rates as offered by the multinationals. There may be no obvious reason to grant better conditions to those who happen to gain employment with a multinational corporation rather than a domestic enterprise, so the remainder of the labor force may conclude that injustice has been done. Where there is pressure to raise wage rates, however, domestic industries may be affected, and perhaps have their viability endangered as the result.[15]

If worker compensation is raised above the prevailing level, moreover, there may be no uncontroversial principle for determining what it should be. If wages are placed at the level of workers in equivalent positions in developed nations, laborers in underdeveloped nations may find themselves enormously wealthy by local standards. If wages are only raised sufficiently to provide a standard of living which is comfortable by local standards, laborers may receive the income of highly educated professionals, who sometimes receive modest wages in developing nations.

In addition, it is notoriously difficult to determine what the minimal level of a decent human existence should be. The minimum in Bangladesh, for example, is quite different from that of the United States, Great Britain or any other industrialized nation. Conversely, what is thought to be required for a decent life in Western Europe, such as indoor plumbing or access to modern medical care, may be wildly extravagant in other parts of the world. Part of the problem, therefore, is to determine which frame of reference to employ, and to acknowledge that, by many standards of human well-being, the accepted minimum income in some parts of the world will be below the minimum required for a decent and productive human life.

Neither can it be a solution, as has been suggested, simply to encourage laborers to join unions and bargain for the best wages they can.[16] For one thing, where there is a large pool of unemployed or prevailing wage rates are exceedingly low, they may be unable to bargain for very much. Further, in many Third World nations unions are subject to close governmental control or, occasionally, repression, since local governments are often controlled by members of the predominant economic classes. Under these circumstances union activities will be severely constrained and therefore ineffectual. Moreover, there is little reason to think there is anything sacred about the outcome of a bargaining process, which can be swayed by any number of morally irrelevant factors. If the reason for scrutinizing wage levels is the belief that they are morally unacceptable, there is little justification for introducing a process which is shaped by factors which may be morally irrelevant and whose outcome is therefore morally arbitrary.

The diverse standards of worker safety and environmental protection in varying parts of the world pose similar problems. Some nations have strict standards and enforce them rigorously. Others maintain lesser degrees of rigor and enforcement, while yet others have none at all. These matters are of moral importance because human life and well-being are at stake. Yet evaluation of these varying standards is made complex by the fact that people who are sober, reasonable and of good-will will often disagree about what standards of risk are appropriate.[17] Clearly, all human activity involves risk, which cannot be completely eliminated or avoided. But there must be a line between appropriate and excessive risk, though this line may differ from situation to situation. The level of acceptable risk of job injury must differ greatly for a bank teller compared with a construction worker or coal miner, for example. It cannot be blithely claimed that various peoples of the world should be allowed to set these standards for themselves. In this context, 'peoples' means 'governments', who may have their own concerns or difficulties which may cause their priorities to diverge from the interests and well-being of their citizens. Governments may be quite willing, for example, to trade the welfare of citizens for quicker economic development or for the maintenance of the nation's economic elite.

Another complication is that governments may simply lack the resources to establish or enforce appropriate standards. It is possible, as well, that in Third World nations the assumptions and data on which standards are established are deficient. In all these cases, furthermore, there may be marked differences between the risks established by a reasonable standard and those that are allowed in actual practice. The matter is tangled further by the possibility that it may occasionally be reasonable to weigh these risks against the prospect of accelerated economic development: cases, that is, where additional economic development is needed to preserve human life and its means or enhance a nation's capacity to do so.[18]

SKETCH OF POSSIBLE RESPONSES

The above discussion does not imply that corporations, or any other distinct groups, have been responsible for bringing these particular issues into being. Neither is there any broad sense in which 'guilt' can be attributed to the various parties, though occasional instances of culpable wrongdoing thread through these cases. In the most entrenched and intractable cases of bribery, for example, participants may simply find themselves swept along in a pervasive practice rather than consciously seeking to enrich themselves in illegitimate fashion. In other instances, furthermore, the official salaries of functionaries and officials may be so meager that they can only hope to eke out a decent living by extraordinary means.

The main guideposts of response to these matters of cultural and economic diversity were delineated earlier. It is the basic responsibility of everyone, whether individuals within corporations or corporate agents themselves, to do what they can to preserve life and its means for human beings wherever they are found. Also, moral agents have a lesser obligation to work to satisfy secondary desires, but may frequently have these obligations overridden by other, more specific, responsibilities.

While corporations should avoid the temptation to make the world better or transform it into an image of their own making, they do have an obligation to keep to their announced moral scruples. However, many of the issues of this chapter are moral dilemmas: that is, cases where persons of good-will may be unsure of their obligations, either because values conflict or because they are unsure which principles should guide their conduct. Therefore the conclusions drawn in what follows are recommendations and suggestions offered as topics for discussion. They are presented without the firm conviction that they are the final or the only correct responses.

These difficulties are compounded by the fact that in many contexts no one has the ability simply to halt deeply embedded traditions of discrimination or bribery. The governments of Mexico and the Philippines, for example, have made determined efforts to root out pervasive bribery but have enjoyed only limited success.[19] Corporations cannot hope to succeed where governments have failed or to undertake efforts at reform unilaterally without cooperation and support from national governments. Hence, their options are to withdraw completely from areas where these practices are endemic; avoid entry into nations where they are entrenched; or else they may attempt to live with pervasive discrimination and bribery as best they can, while yet seeking to maintain corporate moral integrity.

Withdrawal or the refusal to begin commercial operations in a nation because of deep moral disagreements must always be an option, even for corporations that have no grandiose moral aspirations for the world. Where enterprises find they cannot maintain their standards or negotiate a reasonable accommodation for them, these extreme responses may be necessary, and several corporations have announced that they are willing to make them.[20] But, in some instances, these measures may be neither necessary nor justifiable. This is for two reasons. Corporate entry, recall, is presently sought by many of the nations of the world, particularly those that are underdeveloped. Corporate operations can provide jobs, infusions of capital and contribute in various other ways to prospects for economic development. Their activity, in other words, has the potential to make life significantly better for ordinary people and hence is a good.[21] Alternatively, corporate withdrawal or refusal to make resources available may result in discernible harm to ordinary persons. This may occur when economic progress is required to establish a minimally decent standard of life for at least some people of a nation. Such consequences are extremely important and may outweigh other moral obligations corporations possess.

Also, the issues examined here, as well as the proper responses to them, are those about which reasonable persons may disagree. Particularly regarding matters such as bribery or discrimination, which are not so harmful that they imperil the lives and well-being of ordinary persons, corporate policy may have to accommodate honest differences in judgment. The least controversial instance is that of racial discrimination in South Africa. But what is particularly objectionable about apartheid is the viciousness and thoroughness with which it is practised. The more subtle and less blatantly harmful discrimination of Brazil, while obviously not morally innocuous, requires a far less radical response.

Often, therefore, corporations finding themselves in nations with practices at odds with their own standards are best advised to remain and uphold their standards as well as they can. Two guidelines shape the following discussions. Multinational corporations must have a single set of standards to govern all their operations, and these should be announced publicly and firmly. The reasons for this are both theoretical and practical. The theoretical consideration is that agents must either have standards or not. There is no grey area. This does not forgo the possibility of specific exceptions or modifications, particularly in cases where mutual toleration is required or there are honest differences of opinion. However, such deliberate efforts at accommodation must also be publicly announced and explicitly justified. The practical reason for this public commitment is that, when their standards are clearly announced and the commitment to them is firmly established, corporations are less likely to stray from their principles, come under pressure to abandon them, or encounter difficulty resulting from a misunderstanding of the nature and requirements of their scruples.

The second guideline of the following discussion is that standards of moral conduct which a corporation intends to uphold in a particular nation should be determined through negotiation with its representatives and joined to whatever commercial agreements are reached. This will prevent confusion over what standards are to be followed, allow accommodation to the moral sensitivities of all concerned, and demonstrate respect for the moral perspective of each party.

The matter of discrimination divides into three subissues: those where it is officially frowned upon but commonly and informally practised nonetheless, those where it is an embedded part of a culture, and those where it is practised in a particularly brutal and degrading fashion. This last is vividly in evidence in South Africa and so will be examined in Chapter 7. Cases where discrimination is a matter of hypocrisy can be addressed by publicly announcing corporate policy governing racial, sexual or ethnic discrimination and clearly emphasizing this corporate policy when negotiating agreements with nations. Once again, the purpose for this explicit announcement of standards is not to seek to convert host societies to the methods and values of individual corporations but to establish clearly the standards enterprises propose to use in dealing with employees and in relations with those outside the corporation. Corporations may announce, for example, that they will be quite willing to conduct business with enterprises headed by women or outcast classes, or perhaps establish cooperative endeavors with ventures of this sort, as a means of demonstrating their commitment to equality.

Dealing with nations where discrimination, whether sexual, ethnic or religious, is an embedded part of culture will be more difficult. Openly practising non-discrimination may be deeply offensive to members of the host country. Acknowledging the moral integrity of citizens in the host country and respecting them as equals may require accommodating this discrimination while yet explicitly disagreeing with local standards. Respect for local culture may also require that corporations disavow any effort to serve as vehicles of social change, even while enterprises acknowledge agreement with the aims of social movements pressing for change, as with the various groups seeking accommodation for women's concerns in several Islamic nations.

However, guest corporations should also insist that respect and toleration must work in two directions. That is, while respecting host culture beliefs, they must also insist on respect, toleration and accommodation for their own values. It is reasonable for corporations to seek accords with host nations which will allow them to honor their own policies while respecting the sensitivities of the cultures where they function. This may take the form of applying host nation standards to native citizens employed by corporations but applying their usual policies to employees imported from elsewhere. Such problems of accommodation can often be difficult and complex, as illustrated by the problems encountered by expatriate women living or working in Saudi Arabia.[22]

In this, as in other areas, it would be simplest and least stressful for all concerned if there were internationally accepted standards of business practice or if there were specific codes of conduct for multinational corporations. This would provide corporations and host nations with a defined set of standards and expectations and would avoid the anxiety and confusion attendant upon the efforts of individual corporations and nations to devise standards and agreements for themselves. Though credos of this sort would be highly desirable, their existence is several additional steps further down the road to a mature moral order. Hence corporations, for the present and near future, for the most part will be left to work things out for themselves and with individual host nations as best they can.

In many ways, problems of bribery and gift-giving are similar to those of discrimination, where these practices are so deeply entrenched that they are practiced openly and as a matter of course. Grasping this problem requires asking exactly what is morally wrong with permitting the practice of bribery. It is easy to see that where a single corporation engages in bribery and does so secretively, it has acted wrongly and unfairly by competing in an illegitimate fashion. However, where corruption is so endemic that it is practiced openly and as a matter of course by all participants in a market, *that* objection will not apply.

Where all compete in the same way and do so openly, the charge of unfair competition cannot be sustained. Those who solicit and accept bribes in such circumstances may not necessarily have acted amiss, since they are simply following a practice in which all indulge. The corporations themselves are not inevitably harmed by such practices. Allowing bribes will merely be a business expense like any other. Obviously harm will result, however, for the citizens of the host nations. Instead of basing decisions on appropriate criteria, studying their own needs and aspirations carefully or seeking the most advantageous contract, decisions may be made on the basis of who offers the first or the largest bribe; or contracts may be granted simply because of bribes to be gained for the contractors rather than from any legitimate need for the projects that result. The practice of bribery is likely, therefore, to result in wasteful use of resources or in substantial harm to persons where shoddy goods and services are offered because decisions are made on the basis of prospects for personal financial gain.

Another complication remains. Bribery must be distinguished from the practice, shared by a number of cultures, of founding business relationships on personal relationships. In cultures of this sort, commercial activity is viewed as an outgrowth of personal association. The structure of business activity is not based on legalistic or formalistic principles, such as statute, contract, right or obligation, but is thought to be more appropriately based on features of personal relationships: those of trust, loyalty and mutual respect.[23] The conceptual foundation for conducting commercial affairs is thus quite different from the legalistic perspective of nations steeped in Western European business assumptions.

This personalized and informal mode of conducting business affairs is not necessarily morally inferior to that of Western commercial practice; in fact, there is much that is distinctly attractive about it. Many of those who decry the sterility and dehumanization of modern life would find much to admire in a business culture grounded on personal relationships. Within this context, the exchange of gifts is seen as a natural way of cementing and sustaining the personal character of the relationship. In Japan, for example, as in China and several of the business cultures of the Middle East, the matter is viewed in precisely this way.[24] The exchange of gifts and information among acquaintances or engaging in mutual assistance and cooperation is both natural and laudable. While it is plausibly argued that these arrangements are less efficient that more legalistic ones, the quick reply is that efficiency is not the only value at stake. Certainly efficiency is not obviously *morally* preferable to other values. Furthermore, some nations (including Japan once again) that function by this system are neither backward nor inefficient. They are, instead, formidable competitors in the world economy.

Bribery must therefore be distinguished from the gift-giving and ties of personal trust that characterize some business cultures. The latter are not morally wrong and embody much that is of value. Even bribery itself, where it is practiced widely and openly, need not be morally wrong, though it is likely that other practices are preferable because of the difficulties in containing the scope of bribery once it becomes established and because of the previously mentioned risk of harmful consequences for host nations.

A variety of options are available to corporations that wish to avoid participating in practices of bribery. It is sometimes possible for corporations operating in a given nation to band together to formulate a common policy of non-cooperation with solicitations for bribes.[25] They frequently cooperate in other matters, and there is little reason to believe that they would be unable to do so in this instance as well. Indeed, one of the themes of this work is that the moral difficulties corporations face are frequently handled most effectively through cooperation with others rather than in solitary fashion. Corporations cannot hope to reform the nations where bribery is widespread, and neither should they attempt to do so. It is sometimes possible, nonetheless, for them to avoid participating in morally suspect practices.

The practice of bribery is most likely to be harmful to host nations themselves, when decisions are made for the wrong reasons, or when bribery allows shoddiness to be overlooked. Governments, if anyone, possess the resources and responsibility to press for change in these matters, and even *they* are often far from being assured of success.[26]

This is a matter in which, for some areas at least, the embryo of a genuine international moral culture is beginning to develop. Japan is an excellent example. As Japan and its activities become more tightly enmeshed with the international business world, it is beginning to adopt more of the features of its standards of conduct. One area where this is occurring is in Japanese brokerage houses and stockmarkets, where Western ideas concerning the immorality of insider trading conflict with traditional Japanese business practice based on mutual assistance among associates.[27] These practices have long been viewed as natural and normal, but are now being altered as Japan enters more fully into the world financial community.

This sporadic and piecemeal internationalism is likely to evolve in similar fashion in other areas and in other parts of the world. Until it emerges with full force, becomes all-encompassing and self-enforcing, the make-do accommodations and half-measures described above must suffice. The effort to alter existing practice effectively in a specific locale and introduce new standards of conduct is vastly different from simply formally announcing the acceptance of a given code of conduct. World commerce has progressed to the stage where many of these codes have been unveiled with great fanfare. This may be necessary and important as a first step to a functioning moral culture. However, such codes can begin to make a difference only when specific measures are taken to make them effective in a given environment. It is not until this stage that a mature moral order is approached.

At first glance, it would seem that the pressures of ideological practice mentioned earlier ought, without qualification or scruple, to be resisted by multinational corporations. Such pressures make corporations into organs of enforcement of the state and force them to intrude on the private lives of their employees. The capitalist separation of commercial enterprise and government would seem to be directly challenged at this point. But, on second glance, where different views of the nature of the state and its relation to the individual and of the individual's role in it result from a genuinely held ideological perspective, the quandary corporations face is essentially no different from that caused by the cultural differences examined earlier.

Corporations may be able to maintain their moral integrity in such cases by clearly and explicitly announcing their views that such ideological perspectives are mistaken. Having done so, however, there is little reason or justification for them to press for social upheaval in these matters. As elsewhere, corporations should seek only to maintain their own moral integrity and avoid efforts at reforming the nations where they conduct business. Having agreed to disagree, all parties may work to accommodate differences. As elsewhere, it would be better if there were international standards governing such matters, established by governments and corporations themselves; but, lacking such agreements, corporations can often do little more than register passive disagreement and seek accommodation for their own standards.

Concerns about worker safety, wages and environmental pollution can, in a way, be addressed quite simply. All individuals and corporate agents have the fundamental obligation to preserve human life and its means, particularly for persons with whom they have direct relations. Hence they must not unduly endanger either laborers or near-by residents and must, at minimum, provide laborers with the minimum wages necessary to preserve and sustain their own lives and those of their families. The market may be allowed to play its role in determining wages above the minimum necessary for a decent human existence, but there can be no moral justification to allow the market to drive wages below it. It is true that laborers outside the corporation (those employed elsewhere or not employed at all) who receive lower than subsistence wages have strong claims for the case that they are victims of injustice. This, however, does not morally taint the efforts of corporations to provide at least minimal subsistence for their own laborers. It cannot be unjust to provide that which is morally required for some persons in cases where all cannot be helped, particularly when a special relationship and special obligations exist, as they do between employers and workers.

The level of compensation required to maintain life *does* vary from area to area, and the material resources necessary to sustain life also differ from locale to locale. The minimum level required to maintain and preserve a decent human life in various parts of the world can be determined by examining local conditions, and perhaps using the UN's Universal Declaration of Human Rights as the basis for standards.

The more difficult problem is to determine the appropriate level of acceptable risk in matters of worker safety and environmental pollution. A plausible response is that multinational corporations should have single corporate-wide standards on these matters.[28] When human life and well-being are in question, it should not matter whether a laborer is West German or West African. The standard of safety and allowable environmental hazard should be the same, since there is no relevant moral difference in the value of human lives in different parts of the world. Whatever the standards of pollution and safety that corporations find reasonable in advanced industrialized nations, these should apply equally well to developing nations. It is quite true that corporations have been known to seek out underdeveloped nations for their operations in the belief that they can achieve savings by lowering standards in the areas of worker safety and environmental pollution. From a moral perspective, however, increased profit cannot be allowed to outweigh human life, and comparative differences in the wealth and development of nations should not be allowed to intrude.

The ultimate response to the issues raised in this chapter can be stated quite simply: corporations have the obligation to adopt moral standards and adhere to them as best they can while working to accommodate and respect the (possibly different) standards of others. Even vigorous proponents of unfettered commerce frequently acknowledge that corporations are obliged to uphold moral standards in their dealings with employees, customers, suppliers and competitors. Enterprises may occasionally be obliged to compromise these standards in order to respect the values of others. Nonetheless, they cannot compromise their basic responsibility, shared with all moral agents, of seeking to avoid placing human life and well-being at risk.

5 Corporate Mobility

The facility with which multinational enterprises can move products, offices or factories, and capital across national borders generates a distinct set of problems. A significant part of the attraction of multinational activity is found in the flexibility and opportunity which this ability allows. Corporations active in the international arena are likely to be drawn to the advantages of this mobility, and perhaps also to be attracted to the potential for abuse which it offers. A significant feature of this set of issues is that it encompasses several of the areas in which multinational corporations are seen as distinct threats to advanced industrialized societies, though they trouble developing nations as well. These issues fall into three general sorts: problems caused by the facility with which corporations can transport products from market to market, those resulting from their ability nimbly to evade effective legal control or taxation, and those resulting from their facility in moving jobs, plant and capital from nation to nation. Each of these categories will be examined in its turn.

THE MOBILITY OF PRODUCTS

The increasing homogeneity of the global economy has resulted in single global markets for a number of products and in technological and institutional means for quickly and easily transporting goods from nation to nation. These developments have resulted in vexing problems for *both* developing and developed nations.

Developing nations sometimes find themselves turned into dumping grounds for products deemed unsafe or shoddy by the standards of other nations. In some cases, for example, pesticides that have not been approved for use in one nation, because they are unduly hazardous or destructive of the environment, are simply sold elsewhere, where standards differ or there are no standards at all.[1] In a notorious instance of a different sort cyclamates (artificial sweetening agents), banned for sale in the United States because of evidence that they caused birth defects, were simply marketed elsewhere.[2]

In a different way, this mobility of products and the greatly increasing volume and speed of transporting them, along with the ever-greater array of products involved, has made it possible for traders, consciously or unwittingly, to subvert national policy or undermine national military or economic security.

The problems caused by the easy mobility of products result from several interwoven factors. The sheer volume of goods transported across national borders and the speed and ease with which this occurs makes it difficult for even the most advanced and wealthy nations to keep track of which goods are leaving or entering their borders. Developing nations will obviously have greater difficulty monitoring this traffic and possess fewer resources for doing so. Generally, there are no formal mechanisms for alerting other nations to the possible transport of unsafe or shoddy goods, and this absence obviously provides opportunity for unscrupulous operators.

The large number of times products change hands once they enter international commerce and the number of middlemen involved may make it difficult for the original manufacturers products to know the ultimate destination of their wares. Manufacturers may, in addition, be all too willing to sell defective goods to shady operators in order to recover some portion of their costs. Surprisingly, a number of nations, including several that are highly developed, such as West Germany, have few effective means of monitoring imports and exports.[3] In some cases (and West Germany is a good example once more), this is the result of a firm national commitment to the principles of free trade. However, the expense and complexity of efforts to control the movement of products will obviously place a greater burden on poorer and less-developed nations. The difficulties they face are compounded by the fact that they often have large stretches of uncontrolled borders. There are instances where hazardous products have turned up in poor nations, and caused harm, without anyone having the slightest idea of how they arrived or where they originated.

The nations of the world also have varying standards of safety and effectiveness for products. Most importantly, they have widely diverse standards for testing and evaluating medicines. The United States has standards for the sale of drugs that are quite strict and conservative. Those of the nations of Europe are often less so. Recent controversies over AIDS medications approved for use in Europe but not in the United States illustrate that equally well-informed and reasonable people may disagree on the matter of which standards are appropriate.[4]

Disagreement about standards aside, the issue of enforcement is also of considerable practical importance. Expensive laboratories and cadres of agents are needed to evaluate and to track the flow of medications and other potentially hazardous products. These efforts may require a level of material support and technical sophistication which is beyond the means of many nations. Moreover, while there is latitude for legitimate disagreement on standards, there will be some standards which are incontrovertibly inadequate. Obviously, the total lack of standards is inadequate. Underdeveloped nations, once again, are most likely to be deficient in these areas and therefore vulnerable as a dumping ground for dangerous or crackpot medicines or hazardous products, such as pesticides.

It has also been discovered that some products which are relatively safe and useful when used in advanced industrialized societies can be dangerous when introduced elsewhere. The Nestlé Infant Formula controversy is perhaps the most notorious of these instances. In the Nestlé case, an infant feeding preparation devised for use in advanced societies caused great difficulty when marketed in nations where sanitary conditions were poor, educational levels low and mothers were tempted to dilute the formula with water when money was scarce. In consequence, many infants suffered infection when the formula was prepared under unsanitary conditions or with impure water, or malnourishment when mothers scrimped on use of the preparation because they lacked the money to buy adequate supplies.[5]

Underdeveloped nations have also been *literal* dumping grounds when an increasing volume of hazardous wastes, which have come under closer scrutiny in developed areas, are transported to developing nations for disposal. Once more, this problem does not plague only the underdeveloped nations. There are instances where industrialized nations, including Great Britain and Italy, have reacted in horror when they discovered cargoes of hazardous waste headed for their shores.[6] However, underdeveloped nations have fewer resources to fend off such attentions and less ability to take remedial action when troublesome wastes are released into their environment.

Potentially harmful wastes are currently a problem for the whole world, as they are being generated in continually increasing volumes and there are fewer convenient or inexpensive means of disposal available. The problem has recently approached crisis proportions, and nations have begun to join together to try to devise a coordinated and adequate response.[7] The difficulty of this problem results from the sheer volume and difficulty of managing such wastes, but also from the problem of weighing the human cost of exposure to perilous wastes against the possible economic benefits of accepting them for disposal.

The pressures of these situations are beautifully illustrated by the instance in which Guinea-Bissau was promised economic benefits greater than its entire gross national product in return for allowing hazardous waste to be disposed within its borders.[8] In a case of this sort, it is not obvious that a rational individual, or a rational government, would not choose to accept the hazard to human welfare in return for the economic benefit. Notice, once more, that comparatively wealthy, as well as poor, nations may find themselves confronted with choices of this sort, as the areas available for dumping are used up, or stricter conditions on disposal are enacted. To the extent that the waste problem becomes more acute, the economic incentive for providing dumping space will greatly increase.

The speed, volume and complexity of international trade also has direct implications for the well-being of advanced nations. The prosperity of nations is increasingly tied to their ability to acquire and control ever more advanced technology, whether it be computers, genetic engineering techniques, or what is now called intellectual property (that is, patents, computer software and literature).[9] However, nations face increasing difficulty in preventing these resources from escaping across their borders and beyond their control. Other nations may benefit from this slippage, either by avoiding fees paid for using them or by gaining possession of products which would otherwise be beyond their financial means. The porosity of borders thus threatens the advantage of technologically advanced nations and benefits those who are less so. It also intensifies competition between technologically advanced nations as they seek access to one another's technology and work to safeguard their own.

This swelling flow carries another consequence: that of making the world a more dangerous place. Recent events illustrate that advanced nations are having difficulty in preventing other nations from gaining the means to produce chemical weapons. Several nations of the world have arrived at a consensus that chemical weapons should be strictly controlled, but this is counterbalanced by the great advantages which other nations believe are gained by possessing chemical arms.[10] However, the equipment and processes needed to produce chemical arms are closely akin to those used for legitimate industrial purposes, which increases the difficulty of strictly controlling the transfer of such means.[11] The problem is compounded by the fact that these means are easily transferred to terrorist groups, particularly since Libya is among those suspected of seeking the capacity for chemical warfare and is also a known supporter of terrorist groups.[12] Clearly, the proliferation of the means to produce chemical arms will increase the hazards of the world.

A related problem is that a number of sophisticated products, such as computers and computer software, have significant military applications. Nations have good reason to believe that their own national security is best served by preventing this technology from falling into the hands of others. Yet, once again, recent events have shown that it is distressingly difficult for nations such as the United States to prevent these items from making their way to the Soviet Union or other nations seeking access to them.[13]

In all of the above cases, human life and welfare are potentially at stake. They are therefore of fundamental moral importance. Because these matters carry potential harm for human life and needs, individuals working within corporations, both in their capacity as individual persons and as corporate functionaries, have the strong obligation to act to preserve human welfare. In cases where lapses may result in hazard to human life, the obligation to maintain human welfare must override whatever other specific responsibilities corporate functionaries may possess. Those within corporations therefore have the obligation to endeavor to prevent hazards to human life and well-being which result from transnational trade practices. Furthermore, corporate entities as a whole have a moral agency such that they also have the obligation to avoid such difficulties. Once again, these obligations override whatever special responsibilities coporations may have to seek profits or expansion or predominance over competitors.

Most often the above problems are not the result of intentional efforts to cause harm. Rather, they are usually a by-product of the general rush to international commerce and are neither foreseen nor intended by those involved. This is not to deny that there are unscrupulous operators or that corporations have not fomented abuses. Instead, the claim is that focusing only on the machinations of the unscrupulous will prevent an understanding of the deeper problems.

Due to the potential harm to human life and well-being, corporations have the obligation to set standards of product safety and performance, whether for drugs, food or infant sleepwear, which will apply wherever their products are sold. They also have the obligation to make efforts to ensure that products which are defective in ways that may endanger human life and welfare are not sold to unscrupulous dealers who then pass them along to consumers. Obviously there is not a great deal that corporations can do to control the labyrinthine array of transactions which occur in international commerce, but measures which begin to address these issues are available. Because of the possible consequences for human life and well-being, corporations ought to take them. However, because corporations cannot effectively police markets and transactions, a fully adequate response to this issue must come from nation-states working with multinational organizations. The cooperation of nation-states is necessary because the perquisites of sovereignty will not allow effective action without them. But individual nation-states cannot resolve a problem which is transnational, so multinational bodies and multinational efforts are also necessary.

Problems of enforcement aside, corporate obligations are for the most part simply and easily met. They require nothing more than establishing reasonable standards of safety and effectiveness for products, standards which apply with equal force in all markets where the corporation is active. Corporations should also adopt policies which govern the transfer of defective or shoddy products to third parties, with provisions controlling their ultimate use. This recommendation is made by both the proposed UN Code of Conduct on Transnational Corporations and the Committee on Consumer Policies of the Organization of Economic Co-operation and Development (OECD).[14] These standards will not completely prevent abuses or deter those determined to be unscrupulous, but they can clearly be of benefit.

In the untidy world of multinational commerce, universal rectitude cannot be expected. For each corporation that adopts responsible standards and makes earnest efforts to implement them, there will be others who will happily seek profits wherever and however they can. In present circumstances, no single corporation or group of corporations will be able to police markets sufficiently to prevent unscrupulous profiteering. This is part of the cost of functioning in circumstances where a mature moral order has not evolved. Those who seek to be morally responsible will often pay some cost for doing so and will suffer the further discomfort of recognizing that their efforts cannot entirely redress the problem. While these hazards are considerable, they do not forestall moral accountability altogether. Because of the possibility of preventing at least some harm to human life and well-being, individuals within such corporations (both as single persons and in their role as corporate functionaries), who are in a position to seek morally responsible policies, have the obligation to do so. Furthermore, they have the obligation to endeavor to correct abuses or problems when they occur and to work to provide recompense for those who are harmed. Where corporations fear they will be at a competitive disadvantage by unilaterally adopting such standards (where they increase costs, prevent the sale of products for which there are ready markets or leave markets open to the attentions of competitors), enterprises have other options for addressing the matter. Competitors within the domain of domestic commerce, for example, commonly establish associations to set minimal standards for products, regulate trade, freeze out unscrupulous operators or seek legislation to control their industry. When the need arises, multinational corporations may seek to create similar organizations to begin to deal with commerce on the international level.

Other strategies for addressing these problems are also available. Concerned individuals or corporations may seek to hold conferences to examine the difficulties of controlling the flow of products and look for joint responses to them. They may also commission studies of the problems, make the results available to others, and try to gain public attention for difficult issues. Furthermore, the Organization of Economic Co-operation and Development and the United Nations Centre for Transnational Corporations (UNCTC) both have structures designed to serve as resources for those wishing to address issues of moral concern.[15] The objection that such efforts will not be fully successful or that miscreants may escape unscathed and prosperous is not fatal. Partial success is well worth seeking, because it may increase the protection of human life and welfare.

However, it is also clear that the efforts of corporations, whether singly or in concert, will not suffice to address all the issues listed here. Part of the difficulty is that there may be sincere disagreement concerning what standards are reasonable, or differing nations may wish to place different weights on risk, as balanced against economic gain; or, in the case of medicines, possible benefit for human health. Over and above certain minimal standards of safety and effectiveness, the governments of nation-states are better situated than corporations for making judgments on these matters for themselves and their citizens, or deciding which trade-offs to accept. Furthermore, corporations are not well-suited to make decisions about which products or processes are essential to a nation's security and economic well-being, and neither is it appropriate that they attempt to do so. These are matters for nations to resolve via their governments, and not for private enterprises.

While there is room for reasonable people to disagree concerning just which standards of safety and effectiveness for products are appropriate, it is necessary that nations adopt some standards, and that these meet the test of minimal reasonableness. 'Minimal reasonableness' in this context means that proposed standards must at least fall within the range of options about which reasonable people would disagree, and outside the group of choices which all reasonable people would agree are inadequate.

Some nations, however, are too poor and struggling to establish reasonable standards or the bureaucracy required to enforce them. In this case, as in others, the first steps to an adequate solution are found in greater international cooperation, along with increased exchange of information and services. The United Nations has the potential to provide excellent service in this matter. It is capable of building a pool of expertise which could be made available to nation-states and of providing model standards and guidelines for controlling the flow of products across national borders.[16] The United Nations currently has limited resources available for enforcement, but it can perform a useful service in this arena as well. For one thing, it is well situated to contact the major agents of international commerce, solicit their cooperation, publicize proposed standards and educate people and institutions to the need for them. The United Nations can also provide the means to solicit and nurture cooperation among nations in matters of trade. In particular, it may encourage those with ample resources for enforcement of standards and control of the transport of products to lend assistance to those whose means are deficient.

At present, the above problems are found in their most acute form in the matter of dumping hazardous wastes. The volume and difficulty of disposing of these substances increase each day, and are straining the resources of nations, both rich and poor, and of corporations.[17] As disposal becomes more difficult and costly, there will be greater incentive to dump wastes in underdeveloped nations or across national borders, where their origin and nature may escape attention. It is reasonable to expect that corporations themselves should establish minimal standards for disposal of their own wastes. But it is equally obvious that, as the cost and difficulty of disposing hazardous wastes increase, corporations will be more tempted to ignore such standards or, without asking too many questions about methods or standards, to contract with outside companies to dispose of them at lowest cost.

Nonetheless, possessing standards of waste management will provide little comfort to nations and persons who suffer when responsible practices are abused or ignored. In this case international standards, and international cooperation as well as international exchange of information and resources are necessary to begin to cope adequately with the problem. A particular advantage of this issue is that all nations, wealthy and poor, realize that they have a problem and are vulnerable to abuse of prudent methods of waste disposal.

EVASION OF CONTROL

The ability of clever international operators to evade effective legal and financial control also plagues wealthy and poor nations alike.[18] Once again, poor nations are subject to greater risk from these maneuvers. This is because they are apt to have fewer legal and bureaucratic resources to cope with huge multinationals, they will have greater need of whatever tax income can be derived from them, and they are more vulnerable to harm if corporations are not effectively controlled.

It is easy, nonetheless, to exaggerate the scope of these problems and the extent to which multinational corporations create or deliberately exploit the opportunities such conditions afford. The vacuum of effective legal, financial and tax control is another of the by-products of the explosive growth of multinational commerce in the years following the Second World War. It is an instance of where the expansion of commercial activity has outstripped the development of governmental institutions to control it. The difficulties of control, in other words, are not always the result of predatory or aggressively self-serving behavior by corporations but often arise from either simple confusion regarding which statutes apply to multinational operations or the absence of statutory regulation. For the most part, national laws and institutional apparatus governing corporate activity were designed to regulate strictly domestic enterprises and are often ill-suited to meet the demands posed by the operations of multinational operations.

In addition, it is frequently difficult to determine exactly how much harm results from corporate maneuvering in these vacuums of legal control or exactly who is harmed as a result. There is, for example, no absolute objective standard of just tax rates or of what is justly liable to tax. Nations have different standards on these matters, and their standards change. Furthermore, governments are interested in maximizing tax income, just as corporations seek to maximize profit via their commercial endeavors. A government's bounty from taxes, moreover, will not necessarily result in any direct or indirect benefit to ordinary persons. The interests and goals of governments and their citizens sometimes diverge, and tax receipts as often serve the interests of the former as the latter.

Hence there is no independent and absolute standard of what is just or unjust in matters of taxation. It is simply a question of determining what can profitably be taxed and at what rates. Nations do not, therefore, have an absolute moral entitlement to a given portion of corporate revenue. Nonetheless, governments need revenues to operate, and they sometimes use their funds to improve the lot of their citizens. In addition, fairness demands that where reasonable taxes are in place, and some are being tapped to support government, all should contribute their stipulated share. Multinational corporations establish operations in one nation rather than another because they foresee some advantage in doing so. It does not seem *prima facie* unfair that they be asked to share some portion of their gain directly with the government of their host nation.

On the personal level, it does not appear unjust when individuals work to reduce their taxes to a legal minimum. Neither is there anything *prima facie* unjust with corporate efforts to exploit whatever legal advantages will reduce their tax burden. However, where the tax structure is not explicitly formulated to cope with multinational activity and where corporations are able to escape their tax burden altogether, it may appear that the advantage has shifted overmuch in their direction.

The difficulties in these matters, in other words, are not necessarily of significant moral consequence. Of course, some corporations have worked aggressively to evade tax burdens or have attempted to manipulate or intimidate governments, and these efforts are morally wrong. However, since the evasion of tax burden is not apt to result in great harm for ordinary persons, it is not an enormous wrong. Furthermore, as in other areas, nation-states have discovered that possessing sovereign authority gives them important advantages for coping with transnational enterprises. The problem, in other words, is one that nation-states themselves must resolve, and they have discovered that they are well situated to do so. As elsewhere, it is possible that nation-states will find it necessary to create transnational institutions to share information and assist in enforcing tax laws.[19] Once again nations, as embodied by their governments, are distinct from ordinary people. The direct beneficiaries of tax revenue are governments, and their income may or may not result in significant benefits for ordinary people. It is rarely the case, furthermore, that ordinary people will suffer directly in cases where taxes are not paid by others. Consequently the moral wrongs or rights at issue are not of overwhelming importance.

Regulation of corporate financial transactions is another matter of less than overwhelming moral importance. The persons most directly affected by such regulation, or its absence, will be investors and domestic commercial enterprises. These groups are normally financially secure and well-placed to look after their own interests. Local financial and commercial elites are frequently well-connected to government and adept at manipulating political authority to look after their own interests. These groups may have their financial interests harmed as the result of a multinational presence, when corporations compete with their own endeavors, but may also profit in cases where they join forces with foreign corporations. As elsewhere, local governments and those groups that influence them have found that sovereign authority and the perquisites enjoyed by nation-states are generally adequate to deal with foreign corporations. As in the matter of taxation, there are no independent, objective standards of right and wrong, just or unjust, to be found in the area of financial regulation. It is morally important only that the various parties be able to work out agreements as equals, that each be situated to pursue its own best interests adequately, and that deceit, coercion and manipulation be avoided on all sides. The moral issues are no more profound than that.

THE MOBILITY OF RESOURCES

Multinational corporations have the well-honed ability to shuttle jobs, plant and capital from nation to nation. This mobility provides much of the attraction of multinational activity for commercial enterprises, and the resulting efficiencies are among the engines which continue to drive corporations more deeply into international commerce. The capacity to move jobs from areas with high wage rates to those with lower labor costs is a substantial advantage, and one which greater numbers of corporations are discovering they cannot afford to ignore. The ability to construct factories nearer desired markets or more convenient to raw materials is another significant advantage, which drives corporations continually to seek to expand the scope of their operations. These advantages are directly related to corporations' need to be globally active in areas where there are single world-wide markets in order to remain competitive. The means to exploit these advantages are rapidly becoming necessary tools of commerce; instruments that corporations must employ rather than luxuries which they can afford to ignore.

However, corporate efforts to exploit these advantages threaten developed and advancing nations alike.[20] All nations are vulnerable to harm when jobs, capital or manufacturing capacity are transferred elsewhere. Furthermore, corporations have not hesitated to use the threat of such transfers to gain advantages from nations where they operate or to press for benefits from other nations. This ability gives corporations a distinct advantage over nation-states, which may result in significant harm and which they have not hesitated to exploit. The potential for harm in this area spreads far beyond the elimination of jobs. The transfer to other nations of large amounts of capital affects an entire economy. A large manufacturing facility requires subsidiary suppliers, whose jobs and profits are at risk if operations are moved elsewhere. These effects, furthermore, may ripple through an entire economy. In addition, the threat of transfers to other nations can be used to drive down labor costs, reduce manufacturing costs or keep prices higher than they might otherwise be.

These harmful effects are both important and widespread. If no other factors were relevant, corporations would clearly be morally wrong in inflicting them. Further, if nations were unable to resist corporate pressures or lacked the means to bargain and maneuver as equals, corporations would be morally remiss to use these threats and maneuvers as bargaining strategies. However, the picture is not this simple. For one thing, the transfer of corporate resources from nation to nation can be an important boost to the economic development of many nations, and it is also helping to equalize the distribution of resources across the world. The removal of resources from one nation, in other words, will commonly result in a direct benefit to another. Moreover, the larger process of global economic integration and development is helping to increase the economic well-being of the world in general and that of developing nations in particular. The harmful effects of dislocation result in benefits elsewhere and are further enhanced by general improvement for the world economy as a whole.

The above observations do not imply that any and all transfers are justifiable morally or are beneficial on the whole. The claim is only that the practice has good results in general and that the harm caused in one nation may well be balanced by benefits elsewhere. It is well to keep in mind that part of the force driving global economic integration is that many people benefit from it. Consumers benefit by lower prices, a wider variety of goods and increased competition among vendors. Nations and corporations benefit by having more available resources used. Economic efficiency and increased wealth are not the only values relevant to this discussion, but they are greatly important because they are coupled to the well-being of individual persons.

Neither is it necessarily morally wrong for corporations to use threat and maneuver to gain whatever advantage they can for themselves. Aggressively furthering self-interest is a normal feature of corporate activity and of human life in general. It only becomes morally suspect when one party is unable to resist effectively or illegitimate methods are used. At an earlier point in the recent evolution of multinational commerce, it appeared that nation-states were not well equipped to cope with the pressures and maneuvers of multinational corporations. In recent years, however, that picture has changed. Nations have discovered how to use legal regulation and financial incentive to cope effectively with corporations and have sometimes resorted to international forums and legal treaties to press their demands on corporations collectively. Furthermore, as greater numbers of enterprises seek opportunity through multinational commerce, they often compete with one another for access to nations. When one enterprise exits a nation, others can often be found to take its place.

At the present juncture the struggles between corporations and national governments are fought on roughly equal terms. Transfer of resources by corporations can cause harm for nations, but it would be unwise and probably impossible to seek to halt such activity altogether. Nations presently have sufficient means to prevent great abuses from occurring when corporations relocate their resources and can often attract other corporations to replace those that leave. Both nations and corporations, however, clearly have obligations to assist laborers displaced by corporate change. Where corporations are irresponsible in these matters, governments have the obligation to provide assistance.

The various problems which result from the mobility of multinational corporations are not unmanageable. Where their practices threaten human life and well-being, corporations have the strong moral obligation to adopt standards to safeguard human welfare. But the problems examined in this chapter cannot be adequately met by the efforts of corporations alone. The growing complexity and volume of international commerce, and the many opportunities this offers for the unscrupulous, imply that the final resolution must come from nation-states and multinational organizations. Eventually it will be advisable to create permanent institutional machinery, which is global in scope, for addressing these matters. In the past decade, national governments have become increasingly alert to these problems and are rapidly devising measures and institutions to cope with them. Nonetheless, as the scope, volume and speed of multinational commerce continue to increase, these issues will become ever more pressing.

6 Political Manipulation

Multinational corporations are vulnerable to pressure from governments that seek to enlist them for political ends. Previous chapters have examined dangers resulting from the various ways in which multinational corporations can function independently of governments, yet hazards also result when they are pressed into governmental service. As with the coercive power of military armament, the resources and influence of multinational corporations provide avenues for the political manipulation of other nations which are apparently too intriguing for governments to overlook.

Both host and home nations find occasions to subject multinational corporations to political manipulation. In recent years, the United States, home nation of a large number of multinational corporations, attempted to prevent US corporations with operations in Panama from paying taxes and fees to the government of General Manuel Noriega. It employed this tactic as part of a larger strategy of wielding economic pressure to depose a corrupt and ruthless dictator. The United States enjoyed some success in its efforts to gain corporate compliance with its strategy. However, the policy was unsuccessful. General Noriega remained firmly seated in power until driven from office by military invasion.[1] The attempt by Western European and North American nations to impose an economic embargo on South Africa has met a similar fate. The South African economy continues to grow, though perhaps at a slower rate than otherwise. There is evidence, in fact, that some white South Africans have prospered as the result of the embargo, while others have found ways to evade it. It seems clear that economic sanctions alone will not cause the white government to change its course.[2]

Another facet of the worry about multinational corporations is that they may be captured by *host* nations and turned round to serve their interests. The salient case is the Arab Oil Embargo of 1973. At that time the oil producing states of Arabia called upon giant multinational petroleum companies operating in the Middle East to assist their efforts to enforce an oil embargo against nations supporting Israel. The attempt was a mixed success. Arab nations were able to restrict their own production and sharply curtail the supply of oil to the world, yet the multinationals contrived to juggle supplies so that all markets were served. All markets, however, and not only the targets of Arab ire, had to make do with restricted supplies.[3] The corporations acted from commercial rather than moral motivation in this instance, as they wished to avoid breaking contracts and alienating customers. This example demonstrates that corporations retain some ability to maneuver even when pressed by determined governments. Corporations are fated to remain passive in these situations since they are unable to formulate or enforce decisions of national policy. Nonetheless, they frequently have sufficient latitude to maneuver to undermine the effectiveness of such policies.

Moreover, multinational corporations have occasionally been pressed into more active service of host nations' interests. Large oil companies with extensive and lucrative operations in Arabia have been accused, for example, of lobbying the US government on behalf of their Middle Eastern hosts.[4] In such instances they serve as agents of host nations and are sometimes felt to serve these interests with greater zeal than those of their home nations.

The third domain of political manipulation is arms sales. Only the rare government fails to exercise close control over arms sales or to manipulate weapons transfers abroad in service of foreign policy. The careless transfer of arms may significantly weaken both national security and global stability. Hence nations are well advised to remain vigilant, lest their most sophisticated and effective weaponry fall into the hands of possible adversaries or flow to nations that are unstable or erratic. However, their efforts are frequently unsuccessful. A large part of the difficulty is that broad ranges of technology, including computers, metallurgy and machine tool equipment, have substantial economic importance in addition to considerable military value.[5] Consequently the control of products with military application must extend far beyond armaments themselves. This necessity complicates decisions about which products and processes are militarily significant and which are not. It also greatly complicates the enforcement of policies governing the transfer of materials with possible military application. This difficulty is vividly illustrated by the furor of a few years past which resulted from the discovery that highly advanced and sophisticated Japanese machine tools had eluded export controls and made their way to the Soviet Union. The United States considered this equipment to be of military significance because it could be used to make propellers for submarines which would allow them to be considerably quieter, and thus more difficult to detect.[6] Machine tool equipment, with no direct military application and numerous legitimate

industrial uses, therefore also has considerable importance for the military balance of power of the United States and the Soviet Union.
   Governments also manipulate weapons sales to promote specific policy objectives. During the Persian Gulf War of 1980-8, for example, France precisely calibrated sales of combat aircraft to Iraq to ensure that the military balance would not shift in favor of Iran.[7] Its concern, shared with much of Western Europe and moderate nations of the Middle East, was that a triumphant Iran, caught in the grasp of its zealous Islamic revolutionaries, would greatly destabilize the Middle East and threaten moderate states in the area. Other nations have carefully modulated arms sales in specific areas of the world in order to preserve the military balance of power. The United States does so in South America, for example.[8] Most nations of Western Europe have joined an embargo on the sale of military goods to South Africa as part of the broader economic embargo, in an attempt to force it to abandon its policy of apartheid.

THE ROLE OF CORPORATIONS IN WEAPONS TRANSFERS

Corporations must be essentially passive participants in governmental decisions about arms sales, though they frequently maneuver to subvert these efforts, and they often lobby governments vigorously on behalf of their own interests. Nonetheless, corporations rarely dare to challenge governments outright, so governmental commands normally have some effect on commercial activity. From a moral perspective it is easy to reach the conclusion that arms sales should be controlled. Weapons in the wrong place, or in the hands of the wrong people, can result in senseless destruction and human suffering. If Libya or Iran were to gain control of atomic explosives or large supplies of chemical weapons, the world would be a far more dangerous place, as it would if such arms fell into the hands of any of the various squabbling factions in Lebanon.
   Further, there are important practical objections against allowing corporations to make their own decisions on matters of weapons transfer. The major difficulty, as before, is that they are private and designed to seek profit, yet have a great deal of power. They do not possess the degree of public accountability for their decisions or vulnerability to popular pressure that governments must confront. Of course, corporations are capable of establishing mechanisms to assess the political and military balance of various parts of the world and

formulating broad policies to control their sales. The worry is not that they are incapable of being responsible, or even wise, agents in matters of weapons transfer; it is only that, because of their nature as engines of profit and their lack of accountability to a larger public, it is normally imprudent to allow them to do so.

There are exceptions to this general rule. On occasion weapons manufacturers may be approached by dangerous and volatile groups or sought out by an arms brokers known to be greedy and irresponsible. Even in the absence of governmental guidance or policy, responsible persons have the obligation to refuse such transactions, because of the general duty all persons possess, whether as individuals or the functionaries of institutions, to avoid acts which may result in unwarranted hazard for human life and well-being. In clear and obvious cases of this sort, corporations would be obliged to take the initiative, but this should not be the usual rule.

A related practical difficulty is that not all corporations will be morally responsible, and neither will all exercise due care lest their munitions fall into the wrong hands. Some areas of human life can accommodate a certain amount of moral backsliding, but the regulation of weapons capable of mass destruction of human life is not among them. The problem of moral backsliding is compounded by the fact that weapons sales are frequently highly lucrative, and they are often most lucrative when they involve trade with groups likely to misuse them. As a result, the weapons trade is especially prone to attract greedy and ruthless characters. Moreover, in markets avoided by responsible corporations, there will be a vacuum for the unscrupulous to enter and exploit.

Furthermore, if various corporations were to formulate their own policies of weapons sales, it is probable that they would devise a variety of differing and incompatible policies, leading to chaos.

It is practically necessary, therefore, that a single authoritative agency set policy governing weapons transfer and seek to enforce it. Presently that role must lie with governments. But governments are plagued by much of the same diversity and shortsighted focus on self-interest found in corporations. It would be best, if it were feasible, to have an international agency establish and enforce policy on these matters. Sometimes governments approach this arrangement when they negotiate treaties to govern weapons transfer, or they create regional associations which endeavor to set common policies for all members. However, nation-states are presently unlikely to countenance the surrender of sufficient national sovereignty to allow genuine and completely effective international regulation; national governments must therefore be relied upon as the next best choice. Some attempt at regulation is better than none at all, and governments are better situated than corporations to provide this guidance.

It is apparent that corporate activity is thoroughly entangled with national security and human welfare in the matter of weapons sales. The line separating commerce and government is thoroughly blurred in the domain of arms. Governments are usually the main customers of arms, are closely involved in the planning and design of weaponry, and there is a continual flow of personnel from government to industry and back again. It is also apparent that broad sweeps of technology are closely linked to national security, so national policy must govern these as well. Because national governments have acknowledged responsibility for national security, few would question either the propriety or necessity of their active control of weapons sales. But attempts by governments to exercise wider political control over activity outside their national boundaries, whether to serve their own interests or broader aspirations of foreign policy, are quite another matter, and far more controversial.

THE CASE OF PANAMA

The salient recent example is the arm-twisting which the government of the United States practiced on US corporations with operations in Panama when engaged in its economic campaign against General Noriega. It sought to prevent them from paying taxes and fees to the government of General Manuel Noriega, which the United States wished to depose. Both the attraction and the danger of resort to economic coercion are vividly illustrated by the instance of Panama. It was thought that General Noriega was a ruthless and corrupt dictator who was willing to profit from forays into the drug trade, employ violence to quiet political opponents, and shift political alliances to suit his purposes. The United States was intensely interested in his activities not only because of its long and profound involvement in the affairs of Panama, but because it had concerns of national security regarding the Panama Canal.

However, by the standards of Latin American dictatorship, Noriega was not exceptional. In fact, he posed less threat of physical harm to the citizens of Panama than did General Pinochet of Chile before he gave up his office. The United States was willing to do business with

Pinochet, who enjoyed the admiration of politicians of the caliber of Senator Jesse Helms of North Carolina.[9] It was clearly better to have Noriega gone than have him remain, but he was not sufficiently bloodthirsty that violent means were justified in the attempt to depose him. The Panama Canal is a matter of some importance to America both economically and militarily, but its loss would not have been a crippling blow.

If violent means are ruled out, economic coercion is the next most powerful tool. It has the advantage of not destroying life or property, yet may cause significant discomfort and economic deterioration. This instrument was particularly powerful in the case of Panama because of its long history of close ties with the United States. Yet the case of Panama also vividly illustrates the dangers and limitations of economic coercion. The US economic blockade nearly destroyed the once thriving economy of Panama, which will require years to recover from the damage inflicted.[10] It is possible that it may never fully recover.

Corporations were caught in the middle of these maneuvers. The economic embargo derived its coercive power from Panama's dependence on international trade and, most particularly, its position as a Latin American base for international financial institutions.[11] These would not exist other than through the vehicle of multinational corporations. The embargo was a powerful tool because they exist, yet multinational corporations were passive instruments in the duel between General Norega and the US government. Corporations, however large and powerful, can do little when confronted with the full pressure of sovereign authority, particularly when wielded by one of the world's great powers; but, because these manipulations have important consequences for people's lives, they are of substantial moral concern.

American efforts in Panama were ill-conceived and clumsily executed. They brought considerable hardship to the people of Panama, yet failed in their plan to force Noriega from office. While any governmental policy carries some hazard, no policy should be adopted which has a palpably large risk of failure, the prospect of small gain even if successful, and the certain result of serious harm to large numbers of people. The US economic embargo must be condemned on all these counts. Furthermore, it lies at the end of a long tradition of twists and turns in US policy and a long history of meddling and self-seeking coercion in Latin America. Policies infected with ineptitude of this magnitude are best avoided entirely. Noriega was widely unpopular in Panama, and the legacy of his greedy and totalitarian rule will harm Panama in the long term. It would be worth a good deal to have a stable, decent and competent government in place there, and its value would extend not only to the citizens of Panama but to other nations in the region. It remains to be seen whether the government installed by the US invasion force has the requisite qualities. Nonetheless it is certain to be a considerable improvement over Noriega and enjoys a reasonable prospect of success.

The desire to rid Panama of General Noriega, therefore, was not wrong in itself. The failing lies with the way in which the United States went about seeking this goal. Neither is it the case that use of economic pressure, including embargo, is always wrong. The instance of Panama demonstrates only that the inept use of these measures must be avoided. Some argue, furthermore, that America has been far too accommodating to, or uninterested in, other, more brutal, governments in Latin America, such as that controlled by the violent and repressive ruling class of El Salvador.[12] There are good reasons for believing that these other nations would be well rid of the governments that repress them. The United States, furthermore, is deeply involved in these nations and has, as a result, some responsibility for the suffering of their people. Carefully devised programs of economic pressure directed against such nations may result in considerable improvement for people's lives. It has also been argued that governments ought to exert far more economic pressure on South Africa, including the employment of more strenuous efforts to get multinational corporations to withdraw from their operations there.[13]

These examples illustrate that it is reasonable to believe that economic pressure, including the use of multinational corporations to achieve political goals, is not inevitably morally unjustified, but it is necessary to examine the issue further to understand how and why this may be so. If the instance of Panama does not demonstrate that all such efforts are wrong, it certainly illustrates that the matter requires careful thought and that the mistakes made in Panama should be avoided elsewhere.

THE ROLE OF GOVERNMENTS

Three interlocked issues must be addressed in order to sort out the above questions. The first is that of whether there are circumstances where it is appropriate for governments to seek to depose other governments or use coercion in the effort to alter their policies. The second is whether it is appropriate to enlist multinational corporations when economic pressure is employed in the service of these ends. Finally, there is the question of whether multinational corporations themselves have significant obligations in these matters.

There is little reason to believe that whichever governments somehow gain sovereignty also have a strong moral entitlement to retain it under any and all circumstances, or that they are entitled to remain completely free from all attempts at coercion which originate outside their borders. Scholars distinguish between *de facto* possession of sovereignty and the moral entitlement to retain it. There are governments with sovereign power but without entitlement to retain it or for whom there are strong, morally sound, reasons to seek their removal. Some scholars use the term 'legitimacy' to refer to the entitlement of governments to retain their power, but this seems too strong a term.[14] It carries the implication that governments either have legitimacy or they do not. If they do, they are entitled to retain it under any and all circumstances but, if they do not, they have no claim at all to sovereignty. But it is possible to conceive of circumstances where there would be good reasons for seeking the removal of any government. None is perfect. All could be improved, and all occasionally exhibit substantial failures of justice or of wisdom. Furthermore, all can be claimed persuasively to be illegitimate from one ideological perspective or another, whether it be liberal democratic, Marxist or militant Islamic.

It seems plausible to believe that, even if all governments fall short of absolute entitlement to sovereignty, only their own citizens have legitimate authority to seek to overthrow them.[15] This is because the choice of government is generally considered to be the exclusive prerogative of citizens. However, it is not entirely clear why this should be so. The general idea seems to be that governments act on behalf of, and for the benefit of, their citizens and are therefore an extension of citizens' personal autonomy. To thwart their government, therefore, is to thwart the ability of citizens to lead their lives as they wish. But, on examination, this assumption is implausible. No government enjoys the full consent of all. Moreover, any government may on occasion fail to gain the allegiance of a substantial majority of its people. Even so-called popular revolutions, such as that which empowered the Sandinistas in Nicaragua or the American Revolution, did not receive support from all citizens.[16] Governments commonly accept authority to look after the welfare of their citizens and represent them in dealings with the rest of the world. However, this prerogative is quite different from a mandate to serve as the agents of their citizens' autonomy, since carrying out governmental responsibility may not entail consulting citizens' wishes and may sometimes require overriding their explicit desires. Also, many people have no interest at all in what governments do, other than on those rare occasions when governments catch their attention or arouse their irritation.

Furthermore, governments' interests frequently diverge from those of their people. They often seek to build formidable military forces to gain national prestige or pursue foreign policy goals which have little relation to the aspirations and needs of their people. Also, governments in power commonly have a strong desire for internal security and stability. To maintain the status quo, they may trample on their citizens' rights of freedom of speech or association. Frequently enough, governments also become dominated by a single elite class or individual and are employed to serve *their* own interests rather than those of the people as a whole.

Hence, there is normally only an indirect relationship between the activity of governments and the personal autonomy of individuals. If the autonomy of individuals is understood as the ability to make decisions about their personal lives, then carry them out, governments normally affect personal autonomy only indirectly and marginally.

It is also not obvious that a change in government would give individual persons more or less control over their individual lives or even that the change from autocratic to democratic government would give them greater resources and opportunities for controlling their destinies. Autocratic governments are sometimes content to leave people alone, so long as they do not seek to involve themselves in politics, while thoroughly democratic governments, such as that of Sweden, may intrude actively into the personal lives of citizens.[17]

As the governments of nations are not simply extensions of the agency of human individuals, often having distinct interests of their own which are opposed to those of their citizens, and because the conditions of their grasp on sovereign power frequently have very little to do with the wishes of citizens, there is no reason why there should be an absolute bar to attempts to overthrow them. Moreover, it is sometimes the case that a government is widely unpopular, abuses its populace or is ineffectual, yet its citizens are too oppressed to rise up in revolt or do not wish to resort to violent means to press their disfavor. In such cases, popular quiescence should obviously not be interpreted as acceptance or approval of a government.

There is in principle no difference between domestic attempts to overthrow governments and efforts which originate outside national borders because of the tenuous link between personal autonomy and governmental activity. There are many practical reasons why the exogenous efforts are less likely to be successful and more likely to result in despotism than home-grown revolt, but this does not imply that no such efforts can be justified.

These considerations are also relevant to the discussion of efforts to pressure governments to change their course of action which do not include the attempt to overthrow them. If the actions of governments are only indirectly connected to the personal autonomy of individuals, there can be little objection to intervention from abroad on *that* account. Even when individual citizens have clear preferences about government policies, it is rare for these desires to be closely intertwined with the decisions which control individual lives. Furthermore, there are policies and actions which are morally wrong in themselves, quite apart from whether they are advanced by individuals or by national governments. Racism, cruelty, murder and gross economic injustice, for example, are wrong whether practiced by individuals or by governments. In cases of this sort, particularly where the wrong results in serious harm to individual human beings, it is not remiss to override the wishes of wrongdoers, whether governments or individuals, or coerce them to redirect their course of action.

On occasion, therefore, it is morally justifiable for governments to seek to alter the policies of other governments or, in the extreme case, seek to depose them. This conclusion opens the way to resolving the second question, that of whether it is justifiable for governments to press multinational corporations into service as the agents of their coercive efforts. A number of plausible arguments weigh against this view. One is that economic chaos is likely to result if the flow of multinational commerce is channeled by political rather than economic considerations. A second is that corporations are private and independent of governments. It is therefore inappropriate to seek to press them into the service of government objectives and also morally objectionable, because it is a sort of involuntary servitude. Finally, it may be claimed that business activity is built on a scaffolding of private contractual relationships, whether between corporations, between corporations and individual persons, or between corporations and governments. When these relationships are established, the parties accept certain responsibilities and create legitimate expectations which must be grounded on a foundation of trust and good-will. These relations will be seriously undermined if corporations are continually tossed about by governmental policy.

Each of these arguments encloses a significant measure of truth. They have enough force to rule out political manipulation of commercial endeavor as a matter of day-to-day foreign policy, but these considerations are not sufficiently overwhelming also to rule out political interference in exceptional cases. Gross political manipulation of corporate activity would certainly result in economic chaos. The condition of the economy in Panama resulting from the US economic blockade provides ample testimony to the potential for social disruption and personal hardship which such efforts contain. The instance of Panama illustrates as vividly as any that economic coercion should not employed a matter of course.

However, politics and commerce are presently inextricably intertwined on the international level. Export policies and currency regulation are under close governmental supervision. Also, international economic regulatory and coordinating bodies, such as GATT or the OECD, are composed of governments, not corporations.[18] Governments presently accept, and are encouraged in this view by corporations, the responsibility to seek favorable balances of trade, ease the entry of their corporations into foreign markets or control rates of currency exchange. In these domains there is not a sharp distinction between commerce and politics, but rather a thorough intermingling.

The question is not, therefore, whether international commerce and politics should intertwine but how they will do so. However, the commingling described above exemplifies political activity undertaken in the service of commerce. It has not yet been shown that is either wise or appropriate to enlist commerce in the service of politics. Earlier fears regarding the dangers of commerce being tossed about by politics, in other words, return and have not been met. The perspective necessary for a response to this issue is gained by reference to earlier discussions of the justification required for one government to intrude in the domestic affairs of another. Vigorous intrusion in the affairs of one nation by another nation, which includes the use of coercive means, may be justified only where human life and well-being are at stake. The general obligation to respond to such crises is of sufficient importance to override other, more specific, obligations which human beings possess and thus to fracture the usual boundaries between human institutions. Hence, commerce can be legitimately pressed into political service in these cases *if* the coercive politics are serving fundamental human obligations. The politics will not be politics as usual, and the intrusion of politics into commerce will, therefore, normally be rare.

Discussion of this issue points the way to the resolution of the other arguments weighing against the political manipulation of multinational commerce. Those instances where economic coercion is legitimate will be extreme cases of fundamental importance, those where human life and welfare are at stake, and other obligations must recede into the background. There are, furthermore, numerous precedents for this sort of realignment of responsibility and fracturing of institutional boundaries. Private individuals and private corporations are commonly pressed into governmental service in times of crisis, as in the case of war, natural disaster or social upheaval. Crises of the sort where governmental intrusion would be morally legitimate include those where the size, power and influence of multinational corporations can be harnessed to serve as useful and important instruments for engineering change.

The implication of this result for instances where contractual agreements are at risk, because corporations have been pressed into political service by governments, are also clear. Contractual agreements and the responsibilities they create are morally important, but they are not so very important that they override all other considerations. There may be occasions when they are legitimately overridden, and instances serious enough to clearly justify governmental intervention in the affairs of another state would be among them. The contractual basis of business relationships would be destroyed if this disruption occurred frequently or as a matter of course, but business confidence would not be seriously undermined if the intrusion occurred only in the rare and exceptional case, and it was apparent that this intrusion was guided by clearly delimited moral principles.

If it is granted that intervention will be justified only in extreme cases of threat to human life and well-being, those where other, lesser, obligations must be set aside, it follows that corporations and the individuals functioning within them will be obliged to assist governmental policies formulated to meet these problems. However, most often their role must remain passive: that is, corporations and the persons within them must simply assist in implementing decisions made by governments. In large part, this is the implication of earlier conclusions that corporations should focus their attention on the direct and indirect harm which they cause and not seek to improve the world. The arguments for corporate quiescence in broader ranges of moral endeavor apply in this instance as well.

The general requirement of corporate passivity requires amplification in one respect. In certain clear-cut and extreme cases, corporations may have the obligation to take the initiative, but this effort may take various forms. They could refuse sales of weapons or products likely to be employed in ways which will endanger human life in irresponsible fashion. They could, in other cases, call problems to the attention of their home governments and seek guidance for coping with them, or they could seek to bring matters of moral perplexity to the attention of other members of the business community, or of international organizations, with the hope that they will cooperate to address them.

With the tangle of commerce and politics on the international level, manipulation of corporations by governments (and vice versa) is probably inevitable. Extreme instances of manipulation of multinational corporations by governments in an effort to coerce the governments of other nations are less inevitable but also frequent enough. However, these maneuvers are occasionally justified. Such measures should not be employed frivolously or in ignorance. US economic intervention in Panama in an effort to oust Noriega is a clear example of unjustified intervention. With rare exceptions, as outlined above, corporations must remain passive agents in these matters, though they are obliged to be cooperative when such policies are well-conceived and there is clear need for them. However, when governmental efforts are not well-conceived, corporations will normally have little choice but to comply. For the most part corporations are well advised to leave the decisions about wisdom and prudence in these matters to the consideration of others. But, as the particularly tangled and anguished case of South Africa illustrates, such decisions and the will to implement them are not easily found.

7 South Africa

Presently, the most pressing and spectacular issues of multinational corporate responsibility concern their role in South Africa. In the fall of 1986, several major US corporations began to withdraw from their South African operations. Later in the fall and in the winter of 1987, the trickle turned into a flood. By the spring of 1987, most major corporations had withdrawn.[1] Some enterprises announced reasons for departure which mentioned only South Africa's deteriorating business climate and their own diminishing profitability. Others explicitly stated that their motive for departure was moral revulsion over the intractable racism of the ruling class.[2] *All* were under substantial public and political pressure to leave.

At the time of writing, South Africa appears to be on the cusp of momentous change. A new government has taken power that seems to recognize the inevitability of dismantling apartheid. It has released a number of long-imprisoned black opposition leaders, eliminated some portions of the system of apartheid and appears to be genuinely interested in setting the nation on a new course. However, this delicate maneuvering could be upset in a variety of ways, with chaos and violence the result. Conservatives remaining in the ruling Nationalist Party could reassert their control and reverse the present course of events. More violent and less pragmatic members of the African National Congress could become impatient with the pace and direction of change. The more militant Pan-Africanist Movement could become dominant among black political groups, or the rising expectations of the black population may erupt into violence.[3] Either dismantling apartheid or a lapse into violent turmoil would make further discussion of the corporate role in South Africa moot. However, the issues posed by South Africa are of the highest importance and are well worth examination for the lessons they may contain regarding corporate moral accountability. It is worth asking whether corporations withdrew for the right reasons and whether there are any substantive moral arguments to support their departure. It is also most important to determine whether or how the lessons of South Africa can be applied elsewhere; whether, that is, they yield general guidelines for corporate endeavor in other parts of the world.

THE MORAL WRONG OF APARTHEID

At the outset it must be noted that there are good utilitarian reasons for condemning the regime in South Africa. It has been argued, and appears fashionable to believe, that utilitarianism is incapable of comprehending the magnitude of the evil of the South African regime. This is false. The benefits to the few which result from apartheid are vastly outweighed by the misery of the great majority. But the nature of the benefits which the white minority derives from apartheid must be understood correctly. Members of the ruling Nationalist Party are not simply racists, indulging themselves in wholesale bigotry. The reality is that they enjoy considerable material gain from the exploitation of black workers and that the economy of South Africa is heavily dependent on a ready supply of black labor. Without black workers, the economy would quickly shut down.[4] But the ruling party has deliberately created a system in which blacks must depend upon them for jobs and subsistence, while white South Africans enjoy the fruits of black labor.[5] So the benefit to whites is considerable material prosperity, while the burden blacks must endure includes material impoverishment, personal degradation and political disenfranchisement. It is a system which has been compared in illuminating fashion to slavery.[6] Moreover, it is clear that the price paid by the members of the nation as a whole far overshadows the benefits gained for the white minority.

The South African system also offends against utilitarianism in a deeper way, however. Bentham insisted that, for the utilitarian, each must count as one, none as more than one and, by implication, none as less than one. The utilitarian emphasis on calculation of benefits and harms should not divert attention from the necessary analysis of the implications of what it means to count each person as one and the consequences of failure to do so. This is an essential feature of utilitarianism, a feature which, as R. M. Hare argues, allows it to be counted as a *moral* theory.[7] The South African government blatantly violates this requirement of utilitarianism by failing to acknowledge the legitimacy of the wants and needs of its black population. As such, it must stand condemned by utilitarianism in a fundamental way. The most profound obligation laid on humanity by utilitarianism is to take the needs of all into account. There can be no greater utilitarian wrong than the willful and self-serving refusal to do so.

The system of apartheid thus is strongly opposed by the utilitarian perspective of this book. Corporations that have invested in South

Africa, maintain factories and sales organizations there, and have profited from their presence, are deeply entangled in the moral issues of apartheid. The question at hand is whether this condemnation has implications for corporate activity in South Africa.

THE ROLE OF CORPORATIONS IN SOUTH AFRICA

Corporations have clearly profited from their ventures in South Africa. They have found markets and made money there. What is not so clear is whether they have benefited specifically from apartheid or whether their their presence has helped sustain it. South Africa attracted them because it was a stable, technologically advanced nation with a population sufficiently prosperous to afford their products. These factors explain why corporations flocked to South Africa rather than, say, Tanzania. Of the above, only the prosperity of the white population of South Africa can be specifically attributed to apartheid, though it is not obvious that the markets in South Africa would have dried up without this enclave of white wealth. In fact, the market for corporate products might well have expanded if a broader range of the South African populace had enjoyed the full benefit of its economy. Corporations may have also profited by being able to pay black laborers lower wages than if apartheid had not existed. Once more, though, this is not obviously true, as the wage scales were somewhat higher for blacks there than elsewhere in Africa.[8] Moreover, corporate activity has improved the lot of at least some blacks by providing them with access to better positions and higher wages than might otherwise have been possible. Furthermore, a significant number of foreign corporations have pledged adherence to the Sullivan Principles, which demand equal treatment for black employees, along with efforts to avoid some of the abuses of apartheid, at least for their own workers.[9] Insofar as they have accomplished this, and perhaps provided an edifying example for domestic South African enterprises, they have done some good, good which is not inconsequential.

If corporations had exploited their employees or mirrored apartheid practices in their own activities, the solution would be straightforward. Their abuses should cease. But their involvement in South Africa is more complex than this. They have brought capital into South Africa, created jobs there, and contributed to its economy. In doing so they have assisted, at least indirectly, in preserving a despotic regime. A prosperous economy, wherever it is found, contributes to the preservation of the status quo since it removes a major cause of mass discontent and provides the prospect of benefit for those who cooperate with the powers that be. By helping to create wealth corporations produce greater material resources for the regime in power to use to preserve itself. Where a government deserves to be removed, or where a flourishing economy helps insulate that government from pressures to change, corporate agents who contribute to prosperity are one element of the overall set of conditions which allows it to remain in power. In a case of this sort, merely taking care to treat employees decently will not suffice to allow corporations to avoid the charge of playing a role in maintaining a system of apartheid. Furthermore, even where corporations adhere closely to the Sullivan Principles, and even if they make every effort to treat their employees fairly and with respect, the close control which the South African government exercises over all spheres of human activity means that they will inevitably apply much of the apartheid system in dealing with their employees. Therefore foreign corporations in South Africa bear at least some responsibility for the existence of apartheid. Because they entered South Africa freely, and must have been aware of apartheid and their contribution to it, they are morally accountable for their presence.

There is also a more symbolic and amorphous facet of this issue. It is more difficult to explain precisely than other aspects of the matter of South Africa but may well be at the root of much of the current pressure to disinvest. The very name 'South Africa' has become tainted. It has become the contemporary symbol of bigotry and oppression; one which the entire world unites in condemning. Corporations active there have become identified with the embodiment of its particular sort of evil. Furthermore, even far-flung corporate enterprises are identified with their nation of origin, so that American companies operating in South Africa are seen as forming a symbolic tie between the United States and apartheid.[10] Symbols do matter, as much in moral concerns as other domains of human life, so disinvestiture is easily perceived as a symbolic severing of ties with evil. Ties of identification do not by themselves produce guilt, but they may establish a establish a link to wrongdoing for which the appropriate response is shame. Sometimes conscientious agents ought, morally, to be ashamed. Sometimes the morally mandated response which is appropriate to this shame is to sever links of identification to guilty persons or their acts. Only in this way can the ashamed party be dissociated from the wrongdoing of others. Where the wrong is closely identified with the agent as a whole, as apartheid threads through the whole fabric of South Africa, renunciation of evil deeds must be accompanied by the severing of ties with the evildoer.

THE CASE FOR CORPORATE WITHDRAWAL FROM SOUTH AFRICA

Multinational corporations with activities in South Africa thus have ties which generate both a degree of responsibility for apartheid and shame because of their ties with it. The responsibility is the result of the effects of their activity in preserving the system of apartheid. The extent and degree of corporate responsibility may vary from case to case. None could have been totally unaware of the system of apartheid or the evils it creates. However, some may have cooperated more closely and enthusiastically with the system than others. Some may have made earnest attempts to mitigate the ills of the system. Nonetheless, a modicum of responsibility must remain for all, since all chose freely to enter the South African economy and all must have been aware of the conditions there. The claim that they are all responsible to some degree for preserving apartheid, however, does not imply that corporations have done no good in South Africa. Indeed, it allows the possibility that they have done more good than harm and that their presence has been beneficial overall. Even though they may be morally responsible, in the sense that their acts have contributed in certain ways to a system which is wrong, they may also have achieved sufficient good to justify their presence. If this is true, they need not be blameworthy for their presence. However, it is also possible that they may be morally obliged to leave.

If the system of apartheid ought to be eliminated, if the presence of foreign corporations only mitigates the effects of apartheid and helps to sustain it rather than serve as a lever to reform, then a forceful argument for their departure exists. As it happens, corporations are unable to undo whatever harm they may have caused in South Africa and are unable substantially to improve the situation there. Furthermore, insofar as the government and society of South Africa support the system of apartheid and refuse to alter their stance, they have lost whatever moral claim they may possess to remain in power. Because corporations can strike an obvious blow against the system by leaving, a persuasive case can be made that they ought to do so.

There is, in other words, something clearly morally right about popular demands that corporate agents withdraw from South Africa. But these discussions do not address a more basic issue. It is not yet clear what is *special* about South Africa: that is, corporations do business in any number of nations with brutal or repressive regimes, yet there was little clamor or concern about corporate endeavor in China, Russia or South Korea before the events in Tiananmen Square in China and the liberalization of the other two nations. If corporations should withdraw from South Africa, it is not obvious that they were justified in remaining in these other nations.

Some, moreover, believe that there are very good reasons for these corporations to be in nations such as Russia and China even though both regimes are less than completely democratic.[11] As the network of trade becomes thicker, it is claimed, the prospect of war between East and West fades and the people of these nations have greater opportunity to enjoy freedom. In addition, corporate provision of jobs, training and affordable products for the people of these nations is a positive benefit for them.

Furthermore, it may be argued that none of the above-mentioned nations commits the very basic wrong of explicitly denying the moral status of the majority of its citizens, as South Africa has done. While all are legitimately subject to criticism of their governing methods, all nonetheless are working in their own fashion to improve the lives of all of their citizens and, more importantly, explicitly to affirm the value of the lives and welfare of their citizens. In addition, a number of the criticisms of these regimes result from very great differences in ideology and culture which, while justifiably subject to debate and question, can often legitimately be ascribed to honest differences of perspective. From the perspective of Western liberal democracy, for example, the governing systems of the Soviet Union and China are necessarily deficient, just as all these systems would be from the perspective of Islam.

If it were plausible to believe that governmental reform, greater freedom and dignity for all its citizens, and increased material prosperity for all would result from the presence of foreign corporations in South Africa, there would be good reason for them to remain. But before the summer of 1989, this was not the case. Before the election of F. W. de Klerk as President in September of 1989, it seemed clear that no amount of further contact with the South African government would cause an outbreak of enlightenment and decency. Quite the contrary: the government seemed more determined than ever to maintain the course of its policies. Prior to 1989 such changes as it made were merely half-hearted and cosmetic.[12]

South Africa, in other words, is genuinely different and genuinely special. There are good reasons to believe its situation is relevantly distinct from those of China or Russia, for example, although this does not imply that there are not other regimes which are equally unjust. However, even the more notorious dictatorships, often brutal and oppressive, are mainly the work of one or a few people. When Marcos of the Philippines was removed from office the abusive character of the regime he created disappeared along with him. The same prediction was made about Chile, before General Pinochet voluntarily left office.[13] South Africa differs in that its injustice is far more broadly and deeply entrenched. Furthermore, the evil which it embodies is one to which the world is presently quite sensitive, that of racism. There are, in sum, good reasons why the world's attention is focused on this particular case rather than others, *and* there are grounds for believing that there are sound moral reasons for singling South Africa out of the pack of despotic regimes.

In this instance, popular opinion may be soundly directed, but it is also clear that there is much that is haphazard and disorganized about it. It may well be that the South African government is more deserving of opprobrium than other regimes. This does not demonstrate, however, that others should not receive greater attention than at present or that the world should not be more diligently concerned about them. The abuses of the Pol Pot regime in Cambodia, for example, were more vicious and deadly than the worst excesses of the South Africans, yet aroused relatively little outcry. In a world with greater and more carefully focused moral sensibility, abuses of this type would receive greater attention. Furthermore, the world should be more deeply concerned about regimes such as that of Syria or Iraq, and it is entirely possible that a careful analysis of conditions in Chile under Pinochet would have demonstrated that corporations should have departed during his reign. However, as shall be seen shortly, there are good reasons to believe that corporations should not attempt to make these decisions themselves.

So long as the regime of South Africa insists on preserving its system of apartheid, therefore, the only conscionable option for corporations is to leave. Insofar as they profit from operating in the South African economy, they profit from apartheid. Even if they make every attempt to treat their employees with respect, the close control the South African government exercises over all spheres of activity means they will inevitably apply much of the apartheid system in dealing with their employees. Also, while there is little corporations can do directly to influence the government in a positive way, they can, by pulling out, undermine the economy and hasten the day when it must reform or fall. Finally, the act cuts their symbolic link to South Africa. Under conditions where a mature moral order is only embryonic, symbolic gestures have the very important function of establishing the significance of moral issues and of moral action, and thereby helping to legitimize them and sensitize actors to their importance.

The disorganized fashion in which corporations have withdrawn from South Africa, and the way in which moral issues have been muddied by political and financial considerations, as well as popular pressure, indicates that this is not a clear, textbook example of responsible moral action. Important issues have not yet been faced. There has been no effort to generalize the lessons of South Africa in order to establish guides for conduct elsewhere and in other circumstances. South Africa is too easy a case in some respects. The world is united in its conviction of the evil of the system of apartheid, and there is substantial pressure on corporations to leave. The haphazard and frequently self-interested response to conditions in South Africa does not, however, inspire confidence. Under present circumstances, though, it may be the best that can be achieved. Perhaps the current international situation allows no more robust moral activity. Still, the moral significance of the furor over South Africa is not inconsiderable. The very great importance of South Africa is that nearly all parties, whether multinational corporations or foreign governments, recognize clearly that it is a moral problem and acknowlege that they are morally required to make an explicit response.

The importance of this recognition should not be overlooked, for it in effect legitimizes the effort to analyze international commercial activities in moral terms and certainly has played an important role in sensitizing the world to the demands of morality. In similar fashion, the Watergate scandal in the United States played the important role of sensitizing citizens and members of government to the necessity and importance of upholding moral standards. Following Watergate it was appropriate for hard-headed politicians to address moral concerns in ways it would not have been five or ten years earlier. If the example provided by South Africa were to have an effect on the international arena similar to the effect of Watergate on the United States, its importance would be great indeed.

Nonetheless, there are good reasons, mentioned earlier, for believing that corporations should not attempt to uphold more than minimal moral standards: those of keeping their own houses in order, avoiding harm to others, and repairing such harm as they do cause. Decisions of the sort made regarding their activities in South Africa are *not* best left to corporations themselves. South Africa should be taken as a special case rather than as a paradigm. It is a special case because the evil of the conditions in South Africa is broadly recognized throughout the world. Recognition of this wrongness is neither controversial nor problematic.

Decisions about the unconscionable injustice of South Africa were not made by the corporations themselves, and neither were the decisions of how to respond originated by them. Rather, corporations were caught up by outside pressures and reacted to them. Given the fragmentary nature of present international moral sensibility, this is as it should be. Corporations should not take it upon themselves to judge political regimes or make decisions of how to deal with them. They are not suited to do so, and there are good grounds for believing the effort would be disastrous. The decisions to withdraw were correct, as the above arguments demonstrate, but should not have been made by the institutions themselves. Their actions in this case were quite properly responses to outside pressures. Corporations *should be* merely passive players in cases of this sort. It would be a mistake to attempt to draw a moral from the case of South Africa to the effect that corporations should become active participants in efforts to improve the governments of the world.

Even though the case of South Africa is unique in many ways, it can provide the basis for more general conclusions. The lessons verge in two directions. First, and most importantly, the governments of nation-states should make efforts to establish a consensus to determine which future cases may be relevantly like or unlike that of South Africa and seek understanding of how to respond when they arise. There are grounds for hope on this matter, not only because the case of South Africa remains vivid, but because Gorbachev of the Soviet Union has given clear signals that he desires the United Nations (a plausible venue for such discussion) to play a more active and constructive role in world affairs.[14] George Bush, the current President of the United States and former representative to the United Nations, appears to agree. If the two great military powers of the world earnestly support the efforts of the United Nations, its influence and utility can greatly expand; but the most basic decisions should be made by political bodies and not by private concerns with narrow interests, such as corporations.

However, in response to, and in cooperation with, political decisions it would not be remiss for multinational corporations as a group to examine the case of South Africa to determine what lessons it may contain for them and to seek to establish standards of guidance for investment and withdrawal from nations. But it must be emphasized once more that this activity should be subsidiary to the decisions of political bodies. Careful analysis supports the conclusion that withdrawal from South Africa was justified, but it also shows that the development of an established morality is required. The symbolic value of action in South Africa endures. The key is to make effective use of this symbol and transform it from a single, exceptional, instance to the foundation of a regular morality.

The present chaos and uncertainty of the international arena may mean that the case of South Africa and the confused response of the world to it is the only level and type of morality now possible. But it is also not unreasonable to hope that the example of South Africa will provide part of the inspiration, and help create the reality, which will inspire the next step to a more robust and sophisticated moral sensitivity.

8 Conclusion

A recurrent theme of this work is that multinational commerce contains a developing ethics. The level of moral accountability and sensitivity is currently higher than in the period of the first great burst of multinational commerce following the Second World War. There is also reason to believe that the level of moral accountability will increase in the future. This holds for corporations themselves and the national governments with whom they deal. The keys to understanding this evolving ethic, and seeking avenues of improvement, are: human fallibility; the conditions of international commerce; and the circumstances which nurture moral accountability and sensitivity.

Present circumstances allow morally responsible conduct. Companies that wish to avoid marketing unsafe or shoddy goods, for example, are presently able to do so without being forced into insolvency. Companies that desire their operations to merge smoothly with, or enhance the economic development of, Third World nations are able to do so, and several have explicitly adopted this policy. Several corporations have policies to control bribery or influence peddling and have taken steps to ensure that these policies are effective. Some have explicit and effective policies governing standards of worker safety and of pollution control.

While these policies have always been feasible, even in the earliest and rawest days of multinational commerce, several recent developments provide greater encouragement and support morally responsible behavior. Corporations and governments now have a better appreciation of the consequences of multinational commerce and its potential harm for persons and for nations. Each sort of institution has become more sensitive to the differing needs and ideologies of the other. They have also become more realistic about what they can expect from multinational commerce. Corporations have discovered that regulation and the goals of economic development are not incompatible with profitability, while governments have learned that corporate activity need not be antithetical to national interest and that corporations need not be sinister agents of capitalist imperialism. In other words, the polarization and hostility of past years have diminished, opening space for mutual respect and moral accountability. Most importantly, governments have learned to use the prerogatives of sovereignty to counter corporate influence effectively and thus close off avenues of misconduct. Finally, the international community has begun to develop standards of conduct in some areas of multinational commerce, along with rudimentary mechanisms for enforcement.

Progress in development of international standards of multinational commerce and their enforcement is patchy and has taken several forms. Several years ago agencies of the United Nations mounted an ambitious effort to formulate a code of conduct for multinational corporations. That effort has faded from the scene, though it may revive in the future. Recently the most intense activity, and possibly the one most likely to be effective, is that where groups of nations undertake *ad hoc* efforts to address problems which are of mutual concern. Movements to control atmospheric pollution and hazardous waste are currently most highly developed and therefore most apt to enjoy some measure of success. Unfortunately, perhaps, a substantial part of the explanation for the comparatively rosy prospects of these efforts is found in the fact that they have attracted the interest and support of the strong and wealthy nations of the world. For the near future it remains probable that any efforts to control multinational commerce which are to enjoy any prospect of success will require the interest and leadership of the privileged nations. Finally, legal systems are beginning to evolve which will provide mechanisms for more effective control of multinational corporations and which will set increasingly refined standards for their conduct.

CURRENT BARRIERS TO MORAL ACCOUNTABILITY

The current situation, nonetheless, retains features which may discourage moral accountability, provide opportunity for the unscrupulous, or fail to provide guidance and motivation for the morally obtuse.

While it has always been possible for those who are exceptionally morally sensitive, energetic and responsible to find avenues for morally responsible activity, barriers to effective conduct hobble this group as well. Among the most serious is the absence of a coherent and authoritiative set of standards for conduct on the level of multinational commerce.

Though a number of groups have proposed sets of standards, none has as yet been widely accepted. More importantly, there remains a sharp gap between the elevated rhetoric nations and corporations employ when devising these standards and the principles which they are willing to support in actual practice. Various agents must still rely on their own analyses of what is correct. They also lack assurance that others will agree with their judgments and lack grounds for believing their own standards are authoritative. This uncertainty will undermine confidence in their belief that their struggles are worthwhile, erode the support and cooperation of others, and complicate efforts to counter resistance to their goals. Governments and corporations in these circumstances are prone to reflect the uncertainty that haunts individual persons in similar conditions. Moreover, it remains the case that agents will often have to act in solitary fashion and on their own behalf. This undermines moral courage and initiative. Where the prospects of successful moral endeavor are slight, all but the most heroic and self-confident are likely to forgo the attempt altogether. Were a mature moral order in place, there would be community support for moral initiative, a clear understanding of the relative importance of various moral standards and general condemnation of those who violate them. Conditions of this sort increase the self-confidence of moral agents and provide motivation for them.

A related set of problems results from the essentially competitive nature of commerce. Those who hew to moral scruple, in the absence of mechanisms to enforce these scruples for all, will find themselves at a disadvantage when competing with those who do not. Where competition is fierce even the morally concerned may determine that the hazards of scrupulous conduct outweigh potential moral gain. Within a mature moral order, however, machinery would exist to chasten the unscrupulous and provide guidance and incentive for those who are simply morally obtuse.

An additional complication is that the circumstances of multi-national commerce and the number and identity of important agents has not yet stabilized. When corporate agents and governments pass into and out of the international arena at a rapid clip, many will not fully understand the consequences or the difficulties of their endeavor. Marginal operators will also be found who will be sorely tempted to cut corners in their efforts to stay afloat.

Ordinary human beings and ordinary human institutions require experience and time to develop a clear awareness of what they are about and nurture a sense of moral accountability. Moral agents require a firm sense of identity, a sense of who and what they are and a sense that others are clearly aware of their existence and their activities.

Anonymity and absence of a distinct self-image are potent catalysts of moral irresponsibility. Further, human individuals and institutions can become disoriented by changes in their circumstances. The sense of responsibility and patterns of response that serve well under one set of conditions may be poorly suited to address a new arrangement.

Perhaps the most interesting group at present, that most crucial to future moral evolution and perhaps the largest, is the morally obtuse: those neither actively seeking to do good nor vigorously working to do ill. This group includes those who fail to recognize the full range of consequences of their dealings, fail to give thought to the possibility that their activities have moral consequence, or fail to give thought to the moral scruples that should guide their conduct. Members of this group are most prone to focus on business endeavor to the exclusion of all else, not highly motivated to acknowledge moral responsibility, but not strongly disposed to resist it either.

In a number of ways, though, it is now more difficult to remain morally obtuse in matters of international commerce than in the past. Few can remain totally unaware of the problems of global pollution, weapons sales or harm resulting from inappropriate marketing of products. But some may fail to draw the inference that these problems involve *them* and *their* corporations. There are as yet only rudimentary mechanisms for forcing the obtuse to acknowledge that such problems are their responsibility as well. So they may still wring their hands over the ills of multinational commerce, yet stop short of the conclusion that they have the obligation to do anything about them.

Some morally obtuse may be primarily in need of motivation. If so, increased knowledge will not suffice. Their motivation must be provided by others. One of the major failings of the absence of a mature moral order is that there are no established mechanisms to provide this. At present, the obtuse are apt to be jolted from their lethargy only by spectacular events, such as the disaster at Bhopal, or intense public pressure, as has shaped the policies of corporations in South Africa. However, spectacular cases and public outcry tend to be erratic, and their influence short-lived and unfocused. They may be of enormous importance in establishing a climate where moral concerns can be heard, and the response to these outbursts can provide the first steps to a mature moral order. By themselves, however, they are inadequate.

Several other venues also exist for goading morally obtuse corporations to action or to make them confront the moral reality of their activity. Not infrequently, stockholder groups have pressed corporations to alter their policies. More often, private advocacy groups systematically urge corporations to acknowledge and respond to moral difficulty. National governments also influence corporations operating within their confines. Nonetheless, the most effective and most systematic pressures result when the international community, either through institutions such as the United Nations or *ad hoc* groupings of national governments, convenes to address common concerns, as they have done on the matter of the ozone depletion of the upper atmosphere.[1]

It must be acknowledged, however, that the current disarray allows domains of honest disagreement by reasonable and honest individuals. Areas of reasonable disagreement should not be confused with moral obtuseness or irresponsibility by those who disagree. In a recent instance, Mobil Oil reluctantly withdrew from South Africa in response to stockholder outcry.[2] Its stockholders contended that Mobil Oil's presence supported a repressive regime, while its management insisted that Mobil's programs were helping many blacks and were blunting the effects of apartheid. It is possible that *both* positions are justifiable, and not patently obvious that corporate withdrawal is the only morally conscionable response.

The consensus which supports corporate withdrawal from South Africa has developed over a period of years, partly as a result of political pressures and partly as a result of the insistence of black South African political groups. The issue is not so much that of which response is clearly correct, but that of whose voice shall be heard and shall prevail. Mobil's corporate position is plausible and reasonable, but it is not in accord with the voice of those who have the greatest stake in the issue. Without unambiguous standards and authoritative bodies to interpret and enforce them, these differences are inescapable but should be viewed as honest disagreement rather than moral defect.

PROSPECTS FOR THE NEAR FUTURE

The circumstances of multinational commerce have stabilized considerably over the years. The major actors, both corporations and governments, have become accustomed to the difficulties apt to arise from corporate endeavors and aware of the means necessary for defending their respective interests. Nonetheless, several areas of flux remain. The integration of the world economy continues, and the pace of integration is quickening. Hence new agents, both governmental and corporate, will continue to arrive on the scene. These fresh arrivals will encounter the novel circumstances of international commerce and will discover unaccustomed opportunities for self-interested activity.

Several measures are available which go some distance toward alleviating the problems generated by the quickening pace of multinational commerce. The obvious first step is developing authoritative standards to regulate the conduct of all agents in the various facets of multinational commerce. The current difficulty is not a lack of moral codes but a surfeit of them, each with force only in its own sphere, and none with greater authority than national governments are willing to allow. What is sorely required is the amalgamation of these various sets into one which enjoys global application. Governments must also seek measures to make such standards as are devised genuinely authoritative for all participants in multinational commerce and avoid the temptation to be satisfied with yet another barrage of high flown rhetoric. Moreover, as earlier portions of this work insist, multinational commerce contains a variety of moral problems, each with specific difficulties and in need of a distinct mode of response. Evolving standards of conduct must, therefore, address each of them directly. This implies that, as new sets of problems emerge, *they* will have to be met explicitly in turn.

Along with effective and authoritative standards, it is necessary to develop something of the international commercial equivalent of 'case law' for applying them. Means are needed to connect the necessarily general principles in sets of standards to the details of particular cases and particular problems. A fully developed case law would also require institutional machinery for collecting and preserving the relevant cases and the lessons drawn from them. No such machinery exists at present, though it would not be difficult to create and would be a great deal of help.

It is also probable, however, that governments and international bodies will continue to develop machinery for collecting information, providing mechanisms for cooperation and for generating pressure to increase compliance with standards. This is simply because the spectacular cases, like Bhopal, and the obvious problems, like the ozone depletion of the atmosphere, will require it. This machinery is not likely to be endowed with coercive powers of enforcement, authority to set standards unilaterally, initiate responses to cases of conflict or respond to new and different problems as they arise. Authority and initiative of this degree is likely to be vigorously opposed both by governments and by corporations.

A development that *is* within present grasp would be to further refine the legal systems of nations in order to cope with issues of multinational commerce directly. In addition, further strengthening of the system of international tribunals, such as the machinery of GATT designed to resolve disputes of international commerce, is both necessary and important. These developments are needed to enable national governments to cope more effectively with multinational corporations, and also, more broadly, to create the basis of a rule of law for international commerce. It is reasonable to be sanguine about the prospects of these developments because it is in the best interests of all concerned that a rule of law be encouraged.

The above examples of what can be sought over the short term fall distinctly short of a mature moral order. Nonetheless even these modest developments could be derailed by future crises. The same events that are creating economic homogeneity are also generating pressures which sometimes threaten to blow the entire system apart. They could be undone by sustained trade wars, major political crisis or another world war. They could also be undone by events which place some participants at a significant disadvantage, such as another energy crisis, a shortage of raw materials, or a stunning technological breakthrough. The period from the end of the Second World War to the present has been one of relative stability, at least as far as the major economic and political powers of the world are concerned, but that could change overnight. The current era seems to promise increased cooperation and good-will among the great powers, but this too could change suddenly with a change of political leadership or grave domestic political crisis.

THE MATURE MORAL ORDER

Although the above problems loom on the horizon, it is nonetheless reasonable to presume that any setback they prompt will be only temporary. This is because there is considerable advantage for all parties in continuing the present course of economic homogenization. Moreover, the advances in transportation and communication that are a large part of the impetus for the recent burst of multinational commerce are likely to continue eroding barriers of time and space and thus increasing the opportunity for multinational commerce and the possible rewards from it. Thus there is the prospect that a mature moral order will emerge over time. It is worth asking what a mature moral order of multinational commerce might be like.

It must be, first of all, an ethics of large and unwieldy institutions. It must therefore differ from an ethic of individual persons. An order of institutions must be more formal, more bureaucratic and more clumsy than an ethic of private persons. It need not, however, be less sensitive to the needs of persons or more resistant to change. Personal ethics are often highly traditional and immune to changing conditions, particularly when based on deeply ingrained intuitions of right and wrong resulting from intense social conditioning. In this regard, bureaucratic structures may more closely resemble Kant's autonomous choosers than do individual persons, since they may be able to examine novel difficulties rationally and modify standards as necessary.

In the domain of multinational commerce, however, a mature moral order would have to be much like a system of statutory law. There would be important differences, though. For one, much of the energy of the system would be directed toward instilling values, then clarifying or modifying them as necessary. Second, disagreements will frequently be resolved informally but there will remain issues on which people who are reasonable and of good-will will disagree. Nonetheless, as on the level of personal relations, means of coercion and punishment will be required. Human individuals and the institutions they create are permanently tempted by evil. Particularly where stakes of money or power are high, some will inevitably succumb, so means of enforcement are needed.

A formal and institutionalized moral order of this sort would require two sets of structures. *Within* corporations and governments it would be necessary to create machinery dedicated to communicating accepted standards to employees and encouraging them to speak out when they encounter moral difficulty. Several institutions have already developed mechanisms of this sort, and there is little reason why their example could not be followed by others.[3] However, this machinery would have to be in place before one could expect any large or consistent degree of moral accountability or initiative on the part of those within. Most individuals who function within large institutions have little prospect of moving the larger entity in a direction it does not wish to go. Also, of course, they are liable to punishment if they fall out of step. Hence they are likely to suffer considerable harm but enjoy little prospect of success if they attempt to urge moral accountability on an institution. Most persons, moreover, when faced with broad opposition to their views, lack the self-assurance to presume that the standards they wish to uphold are justified. It is therefore all too easy for persons within institutions to fall into the mindless passivity of functionaries. If they are to be expected to display moral courage and initiative, the institution must provide structures to support and encourage them.

A mature moral order would also require structures outside and independent of institutions charged with setting and enforcing standards for governments and corporations. If the major powers of the world continue to support efforts to place greater reliance on the United Nations, it would be well situated to fabricate the machinery necessary for this role. However, if nation-states remain wary of allowing the United Nations to acquire too much of the aura of sovereignty, such agencies could be free-standing, as is the International Labor Organization.

Whatever the details, some such machinery of this sort would be required to establish several features of a mature moral order in the domain of international commerce. These include: a clear understanding of the relevant standards for governments and corporations; the achievement of compliance as a matter of course; provision for punishment or coercion to maintain standards; and provision for rewarding or at least acknowledging the virtuous. Of these, perhaps the most important are the requirements that compliance be matter of course and that the standards be widely accepted as authoritative. A mature moral order can function only if these are in place.

There is nothing inevitable about the evolution of a mature moral order, but the trend of the past forty-odd years has been in this direction. However, the standards and institutional machinery that support this evolving order need not be above moral criticism. Sustained examination is highly valuable, and should be built into the evolving structure of the moral order if possible. Even at this early stage it is possible to foresee probable deficiencies in the emerging order. One is that it is apparent that the process is dominated by governments and by corporations, and these institutions will continue to shape its future development. There is as yet no provision for individual human beings, those most likely to be harmed by the effects of multinational commerce, to play a direct role in this evolution or seek redress when they have been injured. Governments will quickly claim that it is their responsibility to look after the needs of their citizens. No doubt this is true, but it is also true that the interests of governments and their citizens sometimes diverge. Furthermore, there are governments that make scant effort to fulfill this responsibility.

Because of this, it is important for individuals to have their own avenues to seek redress or draw attention to hazardous practices.

A second deficiency of the emerging order is that it is not apt to be a single coherent system, but a plurality of bodies, each dedicated to coping with a narrow issue. Hence there is apt to be one set of institutions for addressing matters of global warming, a different set for managing the transport of hazardous waste, another set for controlling arms transfers, and so on. This is because the world is responding to each issue as it arises and developing means for addressing that particular difficulty. The defect of this pattern of evolution is that it is likely to have blind spots, matters which ought to receive attention but fail to do so, either because they have not resulted in spectacular crises or because they have not attracted the attention of an influential constituency.

Finally, the system that is emerging will be largely shaped by the wealthy and powerful nations of the world. As this book is being written, the influence of the military superpowers, the United States and the Soviet Union, is waning. However, the power and influence of the economic giants, West Germany and Japan, is waxing. The economically dominant nations will play a central role in shaping multinational commerce and the means of regulating its effects on human life. Economically deprived nations will have a lesser role, and they and their citizens may suffer as a result.

Human beings have only gradually come to an awareness of the array of consequences of multinational commerce over the past forty years and even more gradually come to a recognition of their responsibility to remedy them. They have been even slower to arrive at an understanding of what they must do in response. Corporations and governments have been feeling their way into these new relationships and have slowly come to something of an awareness of the values and aspirations of the other participants. In a Galilean friction-free moral universe, these adjustments and this broadened understanding would occur instantaneously. Humans, however, are limited in insight, knowledge and courage; and their lives are ordered by specific webs of social relationships. The same constraints apply to human institutions, perhaps to a greater degree than human individuals. Thus the development of moral sensitivity in the domain of multinational commerce has been slow and erratic and remains vulnerable to derailment. If humans were wiser, more far-sighted, more courageous or more saintly, this process of meeting the challenge of multinational commerce may have occurred much more quickly, or its abuses and excesses might have been avoided altogether; but since they are not, it did not.

Notes

Introduction

1. Robert Reich, for example, argues, 'In the era of global clients, the real creativity lies in an agency's strategic vision and its ability to place advertising globally': 'Global Reach Gains Edge Over Talent', *New York Times* (5 May 1989). Also see 'British Merger Bid Would Create No. 2 World Advertising Concern', *New York Times* (1 May 1989). In addition, see 'Booksellers Convention Gains in Foreign Flavor', *New York Times* (3 June 1989) and 'News Companies Test Foreign Waters, but Only With a Toe', *New York Times* (8 May 1989).
2. An executive of the Italian firm of Olivetti has stated, 'You can find success today only through alliances that place you simultaneously in every global marketplace': 'The Corporate Links Abroad', *New York Times* (6 August 1986).
3. 'Excerpts From Speech By Gorbachev in France', *New York Times* (7 July 1989).
4. David I. Steinberg (1981) has a useful recent study of conditions in Myanmar (Burma). For a concise recent study of Albania see Elez Biberaj (1986). In a more general way, Raymond Vernon notes, 'A country determined to shape its future no longer has much opportunity for choosing splendid isolation, except at a cost most nations would reject'. (Vernon, 1977) p. 146.
5. There is some disagreement over the precise definition of 'multinational corporations' and also over what phrase is most appropriate. The commercial agents of international commerce are most commonly called 'multinational corporations', though the United Nations, and others following its lead, have used 'transnational corporations'. The present work uses 'multinational corporations', as it appears to be predominant.

   Commentators have widely divergent views on defining these entities, though there is little to be gained by canvassing the issue here. The purposes of this work will be served by taking 'multinational corporations' to refer to enterprises that have significant operations in more than one nation and are equipped to move capital, products, equipment or personnel readily across national boundaries. This is an imprecise definition, though there is little need to make it more rigorous. The precision required for law, taxation or ontology is unnecessary for the present analysis. Note that there is no requirement that such corporations be huge, wealthy or powerful. As claimed in later chapters, those most likely to be attracted to, and successful in, global commerce will be large and powerful, but this is a practical, not a conceptual necessity.

   There is also substantial disagreement on the question of whether technology and economic conditions spawned multinational corporations or whether corporations themselves, seeking opportunity abroad, created the situation which made their activity feasible. One student of these affairs sums up the issue nicely:

> No matter what benefits multinational enterprise may claim to bring to any country, they do contribute in various ways to reducing the economic meaning of international boundaries. Nevertheless, the multinational is not the prime cause of interdependence. The increased efficiency of international communication has created the trend, and the multinational enterprise is more a manifestation of the trend than the cause. But there is widespread belief to the contrary. (Vernon, 1977, pp. 211–12)

Also see p. 193 of that work. In a more recent study Vernon and Debora L. Spar explicitly argue that multinational corporations clearly dominate international commerce. Though but one facet of the larger process of globalization and economic interdependence, they are the key players. See Vernon and Spar (1989) p. 110.

6. As three scholars put the matter:

> What is striking about the debate on multinationals is the complete lack of agreement between the sides. Claims are made that foreign direct investment creates jobs and that it exports jobs, that it helps the balance of payments and that it hurts it, that it promotes US foreign policy, that it subverts US foreign policy, that it fosters economic development, and that it depresses economic development. (Bergsten, Horst and Moran, 1978, p. 4)

Though this study is now over a decade old, and the intensity of discussion is presently somewhat diminished, the range of disagreement remains approximately the same.

7. Part of the basis of this controversy, as Vernon observed (1977), is that partisans sometimes fail to distinguish the special problems posed by the surge of activity of multinational corporations from problems caused by the process of industrialization itself. He pointed out that many of the difficulties laid at the doorstep of multinational corporations, such as pollution, corruption or economic inequality, are found in nations such as China, India and the USSR which, at the time of his study, had little multinational presence but all the problems associated with industrialization: Vernon (1977) pp. 14–15. Also see pp. 145 and 192–3.

8. As Bergsten, Horst and Moran point out in their study of 1978 (p. 14):

> The United States is by far the largest home country for multinationals. In 1971, American-based firms accounted for 52 percent of all direct foreign investment, down from 55 percent in 1967 but still far above the 14.5 percent of second-place Britain and even further ahead of home countries whose foreign direct investment is rising most rapidly (Germany, at 4.4 percent, and Japan at 2.7 percent). Second, and less widely recognized, the United States is the second largest host country for direct foreign investment. (Canada is first.)

Notes 113

The above has changed, however, as the devaluation of the dollar and continued lure of the huge US market attract investment from abroad. Currently, the US may be of greater importance as a host than as a home country of foreign investment. See UNCTC (1987) pp. 3–10.

9. As Bergsten, Horst and Moran note: 'Slightly more than $2 billion of U.S. foreign direct investment has been so lost [through 'default, confiscation, repudiation, or other forms of host country manipulation'] during the entire postwar period' (1978) p. 20.

10. The point is made nicely by Bergsten, Horst and Moran:

> The view that the welfare of all, and the particular interests of the United States, required a world of open economic borders permeated the efforts of both the Truman and Eisenhower administrations to persuade hesitant U.S. companies to expand their operations abroad. These efforts were justified on the basis of their contribution to global welfare and security, which would enable host countries to raise their standard of living and move toward prosperity and peace. They were justified on the basis of their contribution to U.S. welfare and security; providing access to raw materials...; promoting the export of manufactured products to a dollar-short world; securing political allies among the recipient countries in a prosperous interdependent world economy. (1978, p. 310: see also p. 313)

11. Vernon (1977) p. 145.

12. Vernon observes:

> When enterprises take their first plunge into foreign waters, they ordinarily move with some caution. Once committed to a multinational pattern, however, enterprises expand their geographical reach with great rapidity. For example, during the years from 1960 to 1975, the average multinational enterprise in a group of about four hundred such firms was adding to its network about four foreign manufacturing subsidiaries per year. (1977, pp. 24–5)

13. Several studies published in the early 1970s develop this theme: See Vernon (1971) and Barnet and Müller (1974).

14. A thorough survey of the attitudes and practices of multinational corporations published in 1980 concludes:

> One of the interesting findings of the survey is the basic sympathy among the multinationals for the broadly stated goals of the developing countries. Many of those interviewed disagree with the critical assessment of the companies' operations. They generally do not, however, question the legitimacy of host countries evaluating the impact of the multinationals on the developing countries in terms of the latters' own broad national goals. (Frank, 1980, p. 144: see also pp. 3–4 and 145)

Compare the finding of Bergsten, Horst and Moran: 'The response of multinationals to the rising demands of host-country authorities has undergone a dramatic change in the past decade and a half, from obstinate and self-righteous rejection, to acceptance, and beyond that, sometimes to active collaboration with host governments' (1978) p. 350.

15. Frank sums up the point nicely:

> With this new perspective on the development process has come a greater willingness on the part of many multinational corporations to accept some of the constraints imposed on their activities and mode of operation in the countries of the Third World. Moreover, they have discovered that the consequences for the firm have rarely been catastrophic and in some instances have indeed been beneficial. (1980, p. 145: see also pp. 109, 112)

Compare Bergsten, Horst and Moran (1978) p. 344.

16. For example, Bergsten, Horst and Moran claim (1978) that:

> As for the hierarchical structure of exploitation that the neoimperialist school postulates, it has begun to show cracks as bargaining strength of host countries increases at the expense of foreign investors and their home countries. This change is part of a shift in power from multinationals to host governments that is cumulative, irreversable, and speeding up all the time. (p. 322)

They claim as well that: 'As competition among investors of different nationalities has risen, any strategy other than accommodation has proved increasingly counterproductive' (Bergsten, Horst and Moran, 1978) p. 323. see also pp. 328, 337, 338–9, 341 and 349.

17. See 'Curbs Give Way to Welcome for Multinational Companies', *New York Times* (11 May 1985). According to Stephen D. Krasner: 'The share of direct foreign investment (DFI) going to the Third World fell from 31 percent in 1967 to 26 percent in 1974, but rose again in the late 1970's. Despite the global slowdown during the latter period, the flow of investments to the developing world increased': Krasner (1985) pp. 178–9.

18. For some years GM, automobile manufacturer, has pursued a number of joint ventures with its rival Toyota, including a cooperative manufacturing plant in California. But, in addition to its activity with Toyota, it has no less than thirty alliances of varying sorts with foreign corporations: see 'The Corporate Links Abroad', *New York Times* (6 August 1986).

19. The UN's efforts in the past decade to establish a code of conduct for multinational corporations receive thorough examination by Werner J. Feld (1980). Feld points out in particular that: 'The International Chamber of Commerce adopted a code of conduct for both multinational corporations and governments in 1972 ... The Organization of Economic Co-operation and Development adopted a similar code in June 1976', (p. 108). He usefully points as well that some 200 multinational corporations have independently adopted codes of moral conduct on their own initiative, and these include such widely-known

Notes 115

concerns as the Caterpillar Tractor Company, the Gulf Oil Corporation and Coca Cola: Feld (1980) pp. 121 and 145 n. In addition, Isaiah Frank's survey of multinational coporations of 1980 concludes:

> Most companies had no objections to the U.N. initiative so long as it is not 'one-sided'. The 'balanced' approach taken by the OECD (which included obligations for both companies and governments) was seen as the most constructive way in which the United Nations could proceed. (Frank, 1980, p. 135)

20. In many ways, the progression sketched here is too pat. A fully adequate examination of the developments of international commerce in the period following the Second World War would require several volumes, and would require delineating all the twists, turns and ambiguities which cannot be included here. The brief treatment of these pages is an oversimplification, but sometimes oversimplifications can be both useful and necessary as a means of providing the first steps toward a fully adequate understanding.

    Nonetheless, two points of clarification are needed. First, it is by no means the case that multinational commerce sprang newborn on the scene following the Second World War. Trade and business enterprises which straddle national boundaries are an enduring feature of human history. See, in particular, the essays in Hertner and Jones (1986) for more details of this history. What is distinctive of the post war era is an explosive expansion of the pace and scope of this commerce, a progression which continues to the present and appears to be accelerating still.

    A second necessary clarification is that there are counterexamples to the development sketched here. The most contentious perhaps, is the activity of US corporations in Latin America, which reaches back to the last century. Little of the sort of moral progress sketched here is found in Latin America until the period following the Second World War. In fact, many of the stresses and strains of post-war international commerce are also found in the earlier period, but without the signs of moral evolution. For example, the table listing US enterprises which were nationalized in Latin America in the period from 1900 to 1970 takes up four pages of Sigmund (1980: pp. 36–9). Only a full scale study could begin to sort out these matters adequately.

    However, there are some factors which may go some way toward explaining the difference between the patterns of US activity in Latin America and the burst of international commerce following the Second World War. One factor is that the bulk of the activity of US corporations in Latin America was in extractive industries, those of mining, forestry and agriculture. Such industries are more likely to spark sentiments of nationalism than other types of industry, since it is natural to view a nation's natural resources as its own patrimony and easy to believe that foreign corporations are exploiting them. A second factor is related to the first. Large investments of plant and capital are required to exploit natural resources. Once these investments are made and titles to exploit resources are granted, it is very difficult for competing enterprises to enter the scene. Governments, therefore, are not able to rely on pressures of competition to counter the resources of corporations. Instead, once concessions are granted, governments and corporations find themselves locked together in an intimate and sometimes stormy relationship. Finally, the role and attitudes of the US government changed significantly following the Second World War. Prior to the war, the American government was prone to unabashedly supporting the interests of its own corporations abroad and pursuing mercantilist ends, particularly in Latin America. Following the war, however, it espoused a doctrine of free and equitable trade. Scholarly treatments of the activity of US multinational corporations in Latin America abound. Two useful sources are: Davids (1976), and Sigmund (1980). In addition see Goodwin (1969) who offers a particularly sensitive and illuminating examination of the relationship between an American oil company and the government of Peru.

21. UNCTC (1986) pp. 5–7 and pp. 26–7. Also see Feld (1980) p. 97 and Frank (1980) pp. 135–7.
22. As Heenan and Keegan point out: 'In fact, 34 of today's *Fortune* "overseas 500" companies are headquartered in the developing countries – and that represents a 48 percent increase over last year' (1986), p. 498. For a more detailed examination of this topic see Law (1983).

Chapter 1: Corporate Moral Accountability

1. This claim is considered in some detail, and carefully rejected, by K.E. Goodpaster and J.B. Matthews, Jr, 'Can a Corporation Have a Conscience?' in Beauchamp and Bowie (1983) pp. 68–81 and by French (1984) pp. 31–66. The analyses of this chapter owe much to their discussions.
2. This view is pungently argued by Levitt (1958) reprinted in Beauchamp and Bowie (1983) pp. 83–6.
3. Milton Friedman gives this argument its classical formulation in *Capitalism and Freedom* (1962) pp. 133–6.
4. This argument, and its implications for moral responsibility, receive careful examination, and rejection, by R.T. DeGeorge, 'Can Corporations Have Moral Responsibility?' in Beauchamp and Bowie (1983) pp. 57–67. DeGeorge calls this argument the 'Organizational View', pp. 58–60.
5. This point is nicely illustrated by a recent scandal. Toshiba Machine, a subsidiary of the Toshiba Corporation in Japan, was discovered to have sold sophisticated machining equipment to the Soviet Union. The sale was clearly illegal and apparently of considerable military significance as the machines could be used to make quieter propellers for Soviet submarines, which would in turn make them more difficult to detect. Outraged US Congressmen demanded sanctions against Toshiba Corporation, whose officers complained that they were not aware of the acts of their subsidiary and thus should not receive blame: 'The

Toshiba Scandal Has Exporters Running for Cover', *Business Week* (20 July 1987) pp. 86–7.
6. For example, Robert Grunts, Vice President, International Division, Whirlpool Corporation, has declared that:

> At Whirlpool, we don't place a lot of ceremony on maintaining some lofty ethical standard. It is just part of our corporate culture. We expect our managers and employees to live by those standards and to perpetuate that culture to our future managers ...
> Let me say unequivocally here: Whirlpool will forego business opportunities if it takes unethical payments to acquire new business. ('Ethics as a Way of Life' in Hoffmann, Lange and Fedo, 1986, p. 103)

As mentioned in an earlier note, approximately 200 multinational corporations have adopted codes of moral conduct without legal prompting by governments: Feld (1980) p. 108.

7. One example: following reductions in federal programs designed to aid the poor during the Reagan Administration's term in office, corporations shifted millions of the dollars in their programs of corporate giving from such areas as the arts and education to human services, and did so explicitly because of a felt moral obligation. Some also instituted various means of encouraging their employees to increase their personal donations to such causes: 'Companies Shifting Human-Service Aid', *New York Times* (28 April 1986).

8. Some of these measures may, in fact, have made it overly easy for corporations to go bankrupt, as some have done so simply to escape onerous debts. The Manville Corporation, for example, claimed bankruptcy in order to escape much of the burden of damage claims won by those who had suffered as the result of exposure to its asbestos products: 'Manville Submits Bankruptcy Filing to Halt Lawsuits' (27 August 1982), and 'Manville Asserts U.S. Must Share Cost of Asbestos Damage Claims' (28 August 1982), both in the *New York Times*.

9. In addition to its joint ventures with Toyota, GM has no less than thirty alliances with other corporations. GM and Toyota are far from the only enterprises who seek to profit from such ties, as they have become a common feature of international corporate activity: 'The Corporate Links Abroad', *New York Times* (6 August 1986).

10. Robert Grunts provides a fine example of a cooperative effort of this sort:

> Shortly after we initiated our first shipments from Los Angeles, some Mexican border agents made it abundantly clear that payment of 'mordida' was necessary to guarantee swift passage of our trucks across the border. We refused, and our trucks were moved to the sidelines for time-consuming and total, and I mean piece-by-piece, inspection. We immediately complained to higher level Mexican officials. True to their word, they demanded an explanation by border agents, and our shipments were processed without undue delay. I can say that we never, to my knowledge, succumbed to border extortion.

> We were not alone in our effort. We worked closely with a number of other United States companies that faced similar harrassment. As a group we brought pressure to bear on an intolerable situation. We could not have achieved this result without the full cooperation and aid of the Mexican government. ('Ethics as a Way of Life', in Hoffmann, Lange and Fedo, 1986, pp. 102–3)

11. Roger Smith, GM's Chairman, in fact made this pronouncement in the fall of 1986. He explicitly stated that the withdrawal was partly due to the fact that, 'We have been disappointed by the pace of change in ending apartheid'; a moral concern, in other words: 'G.M. Plans to Sell South Africa Unit to a Local Group', *New York Times* (21 October 1986). But, it was also clear that stockholders' groups had played a decisive role in shaping the decision.
12. 'Whistleblowing' is defined in various ways. Sissela Bok, for example, says that, 'Whistleblowers sound an alarm from within the very organization in which they work, aiming to spotlight neglect or abuses that threaten the public interest': 'Whistleblowing and Professional Responsibility' in Beauchamp and Bowie (1983) p. 261. Another author, Gene G. James, says, 'Whistleblowing may be defined as an attempt by an employee or former employee of an organization to disclose what he or she believes to be wrongdoing in or by the organization': 'In Defense of Whistleblowing' in DesJardins and McCall (1985) p. 300. Other studies of this issue include: Elliston (Winter 1982) pp. 39–58 and Elliston (August 1982) pp. 67–177; Nader, Petkas and Blackwell (1972); and Peters and Branch (1972).
13. Morton Thiokol's engineer, Roger Boisjoly, avowed that a large part of his motive for vigorously pressing his concerns over O-ring seals before the tragic launch of Challenger 7 was his memory of an earlier disaster in which lives were lost after an engineer's concerns about safety were overridden: 'Interview: Whistle Blower', *Life* 11 (March 1988) p. 20.
14. Both governments and corporations have taken steps to establish these attitudes. Recently a group of business leaders established the Business Enterprise Trust, which has the goal of creating increased awareness of corporate responsibility. The founders claim to seek to identify 'new types of business heroism for the 1990s': 'Group to Urge Business Ethics', *New York Times* (23 May 1989). A few years ago the American space agency, NASA, established programs specifically designed to encourage people to report and publicize lapses in safety and design: 'New NASA System Aims to Encourage Blowing the Whistle', *New York Times* (5 June 1987). In addition, corporations that are serious about inculcating a sense of moral responsibility in their employees have taken elaborate measures to do so. For a number of examples of these efforts, see the essays in 'Part III: Corporate Culture' in Hoffman, Moore and Fedo (1984) pp. 133–247.
15. See note 11 above.
16. Simon, Powers and Gunneman (1972), and 'Companies Face Social Issues', *New York Times* (12 April 1988).

17. In response to several corporate scandals in 1986, which clearly involved breaches of ethics, several business enterprises made their renewed concern for ethics explicit. In one instance, Bristol-Myers sent a number of its executives to a program of ethics offered by Dartmouth: 'Industry's New Focus on Ethics', *New York Times* (11 July 1987). Corporate placement firms also reported that companies were showing increased interest in the moral standards of those they hired: 'Concern on Ethics Growing', *New York Times* (9 December 1986). Both greater concern for the moral probity of employees and interest in courses in ethics were sparked by scandal, including the series of scandals which then embroiled Wall Street investment firms.

These steps are important and encouraging. However, they are also insufficient by themselves. As argued in the text, increased moral sensitivity will be fleeting and eventually ineffective if it is not supplanted by structural changes within institutions themselves which are designed to support and promote it. Furthermore, the moral concern in these examples was focused only on the traditional standards of honesty and fairness. Part of the burden of the present work is to argue that moral concerns must sometimes venture beyond usual corporate standards. In fact, some of the most important moral dilemmas will do so.

Chapter 2: Structure of Response

1. The classic work on intuitionism, of course, is G.E. Moore's *Principia Ethica* (1903). Intuitionism has enjoyed something of a resurgence in recent years, primarily in Great Britain. The movement is associated with a few authors including Jonathan Dancy, Sabina Lovibond, Mark Platts, John McDowell and David Wiggins. A number of their essays, along with responses from critics, are usefully collected by Geoffrey Sayre-McCord in *Essays on Moral Realism* (1988). Other useful sources include: Norman Gillespie (1985) and Burton (1987) pp. 147–52.
2. This point is vividly stated by Alasdair MacIntyre in *After Virtue* (1981) pp. 14–6.
3. MacIntyre's *After Virtue* is the best known of the works in this vein, though Philippa Foot's *Virtues and Vices* (1978) is also important. In addition, see French, Uehling, Jr and Wettstein (1988).
4. Kant insists:

    Intelligence, wit, judgement, and the other talents of the mind, however they may be named, or courage, resoluteness, and perseverance as qualities of temperament, are doubtless in many respects good and desirable. But they can become absolutely bad and harmful if the will, which is to make use of these gifts of nature and which in its special constitution is called character, is not good. (Kant, 1959, p. 9)

5. Note, for example, Robert Grunts, 'Ethics as a Way of Life' in Hoffman, Lange and Fedo (1986) pp. 101–6 or Richard J. Flynn, 'The Norton

Experience from the Inside' and John E. Swanson, 'Developing a Working Corporate Ethic', both in Hoffman, Moore and Fedo (1984) pp. 205–7 and pp. 209–15 respectively.

6. Peter A. French includes useful comments on the 'personality' and 'character' of corporations in *Collective and Corporate Responsibility* (1984) pp. 31–47. Also see: J.B. Wilbur III, 'Corporate Character' in Hoffman, Moore and Fedo, (1984) pp. 173–84.
7. The foremost recent work in rights includes: Rawls (1971); Shue (1980); Richards (1971); Beitz (1979); Dworkin (1977); and Gewirth (1978).
8. Rawls (1971) and Beitz (1979) base their views on the outcome of a hypothetical contract. Gewirth's position (1978) is grounded on the requirements of moral agency, while Shue's position (1980) lays its foundation on the basic needs of human beings.
9. Feinberg (1973) pp. 66–7 and 94–7.
10. Dworkin's 'right to equal concern and respect' is elaborated most fully in *Taking Rights Seriously*, pp. 180–3 and 272–8.
11. Feinberg (1973) pp. 66–7.
12. Hare (1981).
13. The author's *Ethics for a Shrinking World* (1990) pp. 12–40 has a more detailed examination of these issues.
14. There is an international understanding that nations should seek the goal of giving 0.7 percent of their gross national product in foreign assistance, a goal few have achieved. Even this modest effort could make a considerable difference for those in the underdeveloped nations of the world: Arnesen (1983) p. 127.
15. Once again, these matters are examined in greater detail in Elfstrom (1990) pp. 14–5 and 26–30.
16. The best and most thorough analysis of these matters is provided by David Luban (1988) pp. 104–47.
17. See Sampson (1975) pp. 230–59 and 299–318.
18. Sampson (1973) and Sobel (1982) pp. 302–35 and 349.
19. As Werner J. Feld notes,

> Some large corporations such as Royal Dutch-Shell or Standard Oil of New Jersey have set up large-scale organizations resembling the foreign ministries of national governments. These organizations engage in carefully coordinated information and intelligence-gathering operations through a network of representatives in the major capitals of the world. At the same time these representatives are used to present their companies' viewpoints on pertinent issues to the national governments in whose countries they are stationed and seek to influence national decision makers in the direction desired by the corporation management. Periodically, these representatives are called back to headquarters to discuss 'foreign policy' problems and to receive new instructions. (1980, pp. 32–3)

20. Friedman (1970) pp. 32–3 and 122 ff. and also, of course, Friedman (1962).
21. This view is stated with particular vigor by Levitt (1958).

Chapter 3: Corporate Size and Power

1. A recent study by the UNCTC observes:

    The most notable result of the current strategies being adopted by transnational corporations is the trend towards heightened oligopoly in an increasing number of sectors and industries. In some areas, modern technologies, mainly in the area of transportation, communications and information, have contributed to the growth of smaller companies, but this trend has been overwhelmed by the growth of large global corporations and the close co-operation between them. (1987, p. 20)

    Raymond Vernon, who has examined these matters as thoroughly as anyone, states: 'In the case of U.S. firms, multinational enterprises have been about three times the size of national enterprises on the average, according to unpublished data of the Harvard Multinational Enterprise Project' (1977) p. 220 n.

2. Indeed, two historians of multinational commerce point out that: 'The small economies of Europe produced a disproportionately large number of MNEs [Multinational Enterprises] before, and indeed after the Second World War'; P. Hertner and G. Jones, 'Multinationals: Theory and History' in Hertner and Jones (1986) p. 8. Raymond Vernon notes this phenomenon as well, (1977) p. 9, and also points out that: 'For the past decade or two the firms that we have called multinational enterprises characteristically have seen their foreign sales grow faster than their sales at home' (p. 20).

3. An analysis of the UNCTC contains the observation that: 'There are several forces that are prompting co-operation among transnational corporations, rather than the common perception of tense rivalry between them' (1987) p. 16: see also p. 18. Furthermore, as Werner J. Feld notes:

    To make the lobbying process [of multinational corporations] effective and successful, a variety of frequently overlapping coalitions have to be formed. These coalitions are not limited to transnational groups, but may reach regional and worldwide dimensions. They may be formed vertically, embracing the MNC's customers as well as suppliers and trade associations and they may reach out horizontally to companies with related or common interests and, again, their trade associations. (1980 p. 33)

4. It is commonly known that the great bulk of multinational investment and activity, at least in the years since the Second World War, has been in the advanced industrialised nations. See Feld, (1980) pp. 10 and 20. He also notes, writing in 1980, that: 'The ties between MNC's and Third World countries are most intense in Latin America, followed by Asia and Africa' (p. 6). Nonetheless, as Feld emphasizes, the difficulties posed by

multinational corporations are felt most acutely in the smaller and poorer nations (p. 20).

5. For instance, governments actively negotiate with one another to achieve favorable tariff rates or remove other impediments to the sale of the products of native corporations. They also work to establish currency exchange rates which are favorable to the export of their goods. The efforts of various governments to assist native corporations and encourage export are analyzed in the articles collected by Nau (1989). R. Vernon and D.L. Spar include an analysis of the efforts of the US government to arrange favorable trade conditions for American corporations in *Beyond Globalism: Remaking American Foreign Policy* (1989) pp. 109–39.

6. See A.K. Ahmed, 'The Bhopal Tragedy: The Failure of Corporate Responsibility', p. 345; P. Shrivastava, 'Unethical Fallout From Technical Decisions', p. 350; and G. Edwards, 'The Bhopal Tragedy: Some Implications and Guidelines for Multinational Businesses' for confirmation of these figures, as well as further analysis of the causes and implications of the tragedy. These articles are collected in Hoffman, Lange and Fedo (1986).

7. 'Bhopal Payments Set at $470 Million for Union Carbide', *New York Times* (15 February 1989).

8. In 'Plaintiffs Faced Major Hurdles' a reporter for the *New York Times* (15 February 1989) quotes one authority as follows: 'Frances E. McGovern, a professor at the University of Alabama School of Law, said that American courts offer among the highest awards of any judicial system in the world.' The reporter also notes: 'Indian law, which derives from British Common Law, has a much stricter standard of liability and causation than American law, severely limiting the kinds of cases plaintiffs can bring.'

9. This point is underscored in striking fashion by an affidavit given by an expert witness summoned by the counsel for the government of India. Professor Mark Galanter, an expert on the Indian legal system with long experience, asserted:

> There is a total absence of any tort law dealing with complex industrial processes. As surveys show, there is no law that deals with high technology or any complex manufacturing processes. This absence results in a lack of the procedural and fact-finding devices necessary to gather, marshal, present and assess data about complex technology; these are reflected in a total absence of relevant experience by lawyers and judges. (Boxi and Paul, 1986, p.183)

Also note, Ahmed, p. 348 and Edwards, p. 360, both in Hoffmann, Lange and Fedo (1986)..

10. This point is dramatically affirmed in a memorandum filed by council for the Indian government. The plaintiff claimed:

> The Indian system, with its lack of specialization in the bar, no fund of tort law experience in the bar or the judiciary, inadequate procedural

devices and no investigative skills or resources, is incapable of accomplishing this effort. Plaintiff's chosen forum [i.e., the courts of the United States] is the only one whose rules and practices will be responsive to the demands of this litigation. (Boxi and Paul, 1986 p. 90)

See also pp. 83–90 and the affidavit of Professor Marc Galanter, pp. 162–221.
11. See 'Curbs Give Way to Welcome for Multinational Corporations', *New York Times* (11 May 1985).
12. UNCTC (1987) pp. 63–4. Furthermore, as J.E. Spero notes:

Until the beginning of the debt crisis in 1982, developing countries were active borrowers in international banking markets, which provided a major share of financing for growth. Although most debtors continued to be able to borrow to finance trade, more and more they were unable to obtain new term lending for development projects. And because of their diminished creditworthiness, most developing-country borrowers have not been major players in the new securitized global markets of the 1980s. (1988/89) p. 120.

13. Ajami (1988/89) pp. 135–55, especially pp. 146–50.
14. Feld, (1980) p. 22 and 93.
15. Frank (1980), p. 41.
16. Frank refers to this as 'scapegoating' (1980) pp. 28–9. Raymond Vernon also notes the inescapable visibility and vulnerability which attaches to multinationals simply because they are foreign (1977) p. 145. An excellent example of the policy of seeking confrontation with a multinational corporation in order to serve other political ends is provided in Richard N. Goodwin's perceptive and nuanced sketch of the volatile relationship between the government of Peru and the International Petroleum Company: see 'Letter From Peru', *New Yorker* 45 (17 May 1969) pp. 41–6+.
17. Raymond Vernon captures the mood of developing nations nicely:

Most of the hundred or so countries of the developing world think of themselves as new nations. Most of the countries on the African Continent are literally new. For many of the others, the sense of newness reflects mainly a feeling that they may be for the first time in a position to shape their own future (1977, p. 140). Also see Frank (1980) pp. 2–3 and Feld (1980) p. 61.

18. The newly elected President of Argentina, Carlos Saúl Menem, a member of the Peronist party with strong ties to labor and a generally socialist ideology, has adopted a plan for economic recovery devised by a local conglomerate, Bunge & Born, and has recruited officers of the firm to serve as economic planners in his government: 'Inflation Unites Peronists and a "Capitalist Beast"', *New York Times* (7 August 1989).
19. Isaiah Frank is able to provide several examples of policies designed to avoid harming local economies.

The British tend to invest only in sizeable markets that are not already being served by effective local producers. One firm has actually moved out of areas of production as indigenous enterprises have become able to compete. The Japanese do not produce goods that would compete with locally made products in the local market; instead, they manufacture for the Japanese and other markets. (1980, p. 45)

'One high-technology transnational limits assignments to individual subcontractors so that no more than 20 percent of their business is with the firm. Thus, when the corporation "hits a slump," the economic damage to the subcontractor is limited' (1980) p. 92. Frank also offers another important bit of information. He notes that:

Investment decisions are based primarily on the personal judgments of the firm's chief executive and board members. They take many factors, including risk, potential profitability, and stockholder reaction into account. In certain cases, public opinion is important. Several companies have curtailed or abandoned projects because of the fear of public backlash both at home and in important third-world markets. (1980, p. 131)

The striking feature of this description is that it shows how executives weigh a variety of factors in making decisions, and that the outcome is a matter of judgment which is far more nuanced than the single-minded pursuit of profit. It demonstrates, in other words, that there is no great barrier to adding the weight of moral concerns into this already complex equation.

20. The activities and policies of the IMF have been the focus of heated discussion for some years now. There is doubt as to whether the restrictions it demands as conditions for receiving loan assistance are justified or perhaps counterproductive. Studies of these issues abound. Two recent examples are Myers (1987) and Sidell (1988). In fact, a recent report of the United Nations Conference on Trade and Development concludes that the often draconian austerity measures imposed by the IMF frequently produce no benefit at all: 'U.N. Report Faults I.M.F. Austerity Requirements', *New York Times* (6 September 1989). 'The World Bank is the single greatest source of funds for the nations of the third world, and takes the matter of guiding national economic development in fruitful directions very seriously': 'Bad Debt Rose Sharply at I.M.F. Last Year', *New York Times* (15 September 1989). Nonetheless, a recent official survey of its efforts devoted only a few pages to the topic of multinational corporate activity, pp. 201–3, in a volume of nearly 600 pp. It seems reasonable to presume that it could usefully devote more attention to this very important and difficult matter: Baum and Tolbert (1985).
21. See, for example, UNCTC (1983).
22. In fact, François Mitterrand, President of France, sought to direct the attention of the Group of Seven world economic powers to these matters at their annual meeting in July 1989, which was held in Paris. Specifically, Mitterrand called for a North–South summit to discuss

Notes

debt and development problems: 'Summit's Leaders Focus on Debt, Drugs and Ecology', *New York Times* (15 July 1989). His proposals received a polite but unenthusiastic response, although it is clear that the world's most powerful economies are capable of doing a great deal to assist in coping with the economic problems of underdeveloped nations. Certainly, little can be achieved without them: 'Summit Debate: How to Help the Poorer Nations', *New York Times* (15 July 1989).

23. Frank, (1980) p. 106.
24. The UN's Department of Economic and Social Affairs already has means for providing aid of various sorts to nations seeking help in coping with multinational corporations. No major change would be required to include assistance in internal legal matters as well. See Feld, (1980) pp. 122–3. Furthermore, there are presently institutions that provide venues for settling disputes between corporations and host nations. These are highly useful for certain types of problems and could perhaps be expanded to assist in others. Among these are the International Centre for the Settlement of Investment Disputes created by the World Bank some years ago (Frank 1980, p. 141) and the International Chamber of Commerce's Court of Arbitration, which was established early in this century (Feld, 1980, p. 112).
25. 'Bhopal Payments Set at $470 Million for Union Carbide', *New York Times* (15 February 1989).

Chapter 4: Cultural and Economic Diversity

1. According to surveys conducted by Isaiah Frank: 'Companies said they generally assume that local laws will apply in case of disputes; in fact, they actually prefer this arrangement' (1980) p. 106.
2. Minai (1981) pp. 205–24. For somewhat more traditional views, which nonetheless emphasize the equality of the sexes and discuss possible roles for women in commerce, see Rahman (1986).
3. Mernissi (1987) pp. 165–77; Minai (1981) pp. 225–45; 'Women in Saudi Arabia Win Some Quiet Battles', *New York Times* (26 April 1989); Esposito (1987) pp. 174–5; and 'Pakistan Women Take Lead In Drive Against Islamization', *New York Times* (17 June 1988).
4. See Lebra, Paulson and Powers (1976); Condon (1985) especially pp. 179–291; 'For Japan's Working Women, a Slow Recognition', *New York Times* (4 December 1988); and United Nations Commission for Latin America (1983).
5. The outcast class in Japan is called *eta* or, more commonly, *burakumin*. See Reischauer (1988) p. 35 or Forbes (1975) pp. 45–8. The outcast classes in India are known as 'untouchables' or, following the suggestion of Mahatma Gandhi, *harijan*, and remain the victims of violence and disdain: Joshi, (1986) and Mahar (1972).
6. Mitchell (1967); Reischauer (1974); and 'They Call Japan Home, but Are Hardly at Home', *New York Times* (1 February 1988).
7. 'Brazil's Blacks Feel Prejudice 100 Years After Slavery's End', *New York Times* (14 May 1988).

8. 'In Mexico, the Graft Loosens Its Grip', *New York Times* (17 April 1987) and 'Aquino's Moral Tone: Is Anybody Listening?', *New York Times* (30 October 1986).
9. 'Eastern Europe: Its Lure and Hurdles', *New York Times* (18 December 1989) and 'Communism in Turmoil', *Business Week* (5 June 1989) pp. 34–41+, especially 51 and 64. In China, even after the tragic repression of the student campaign for political liberalization, corporations responded with a cautious pause in their activities rather than flight or the severing of ties: 'Has Beijing Burned Its Bridges With Business?', *Business Week* (19 June 1989) pp. 32-3.
10. See, for example, Esposito, (1987) pp. 152–210 and 275–301.
11. At present, China, the Soviet Union and the rapidly changing nations of Eastern European are eager to establish joint ventures with Western corporations and are willing to accommodate them. However, commentators point out that in all these nations, the state retains control of the economy and the conditions of life and labor. Furthermore, while the Soviet Union and Eastern European nations are presently liberalizing their systems of government, all recognize that these changes are fragile and that the systems could quickly revert to the totalitarian practices of past years. The tenuous connection between democracy and economic liberalization in China, along with the events in Tiananmen Square in the summer of 1989, vividly confirm this.

    Changes in Soviet policy designed to facilitate foreign commerce are outlined by Bubnov (1987). Also see Knight (1987).

    The tenuous nature of Gorbachev's position and of his economic and social reforms is examined by Reddaway (1989) pp. 19–24.

    The fragility of Chinese efforts to balance economic openness and reform against political stagnation is recognized in scholarly works published before the events in Tiananmen Square. Benedict Stavis (1988) notes: 'China's political system does not rest well with economic and social needs. Therefore, its legitimacy is fragile. This is due both to an unavoidable aging process of the Chinese revolution and to specific policy mistakes' (p. 130). Also note the analyses contained in Benewick and Wingrove (1988).

    For an analysis of the turmoil in China in the summer of 1989 and a reaffirmation of the totalitarian nature of its political system see: MacFarquhar (1989) pp. 8–10; Leys (1989) p. 29; and Schell (1989) pp. 32–3.
12. Daniel Pipes makes the point nicely: 'Muslim activism almost always involves working for the goals of the *sharī^{c}a*, the sacred law of Islam. The *sharī^{c}a*, a legal structure without equivalent in Christianity, is therefore the key to understanding Islamic activism' (p. 36); 'Oil Wealth and Islamic Resurgence', in Dessouki, 1988, and: 'A devout Muslim makes hardly a move without confronting precepts of *sharī^{c}a*; they touch on most of his daily routine, including his eating habits and his familial and social relations. In the public domain, they cover taxation, justice, political authority and warfare' (Dessouki, 1988) p. 36. Pipes also offers an illuminating discussion here of the ways in which Islam has shaped the policies of Saudi Arabia and Libya and in which these nations have used their oil wealth to pursue Islamic goals. Wilson explains how Islamic law

shapes business practice in *Islamic Business: Theory and Practice* (1985) pp. 11–15, and Rodinson (1978) offers a broader examination of the relation between Islam and commercial activity, particularly pp. 76–184.

13. As one student of the Soviet Union forcefully observes:

    All business in the Soviet Union is owned by the state. There is no such thing as private enterprise ... This causes a good deal of problems because not only is everything owned by the state, but the state explicitly claims a monopoly on foreign trade and requires that foreign trade be conducted only through the Ministry of Foreign Trade. M. Goldman, 'How Things Work in Moscow' in Westshore, Inc. (1978) p. 102.

    While Goldman's observation is now somewhat out of date, the Soviet Union still allows private business activity only on a small scale. Furthermore, as pointed out in note 11, *perestroika* remains fragile and is still vulnerable to a resurgence of the Stalinist practices of past years. Indeed, as Andrei Sakharov (1989) argued, Mikhail Gorbachev is seeking to accomplish the goals of *perestroika* by concentrating more power under central control (pp.25–6). The present liberal practices, in other words, could be overturned very quickly and be replaced by Stalinist ideology. Business enterprises caught in such a change could find their conditions of operation very different from at present and could find themselves pressed into the service of ideological goals.

14. The salient example of this is seen in the efforts of various Islamic countries to enlist corporations in an economic boycott of Israel and the more widely appreciated Arab Oil Embargo of 1973. Anthony Sampson offers one of the more readable and vivid accounts of these struggles in *The Seven Sisters* (1975).
15. Baum and Tolbert (1985) pp. 427–8 and UNCTC (1983) pp. 226–7.
16. H. Shue, 'Transnational Transgressions' in T. Regan (1983) pp. 271–291.
17. Shrader-Frechette (1985) and Lowrance (1976). In addition, for several discussions of these issues, from within the context of medical practice but addressed to the more general moral difficulties, see Humber and Almeder (1987).
18. This issue is illustrated in especially poignant fashion by an item in a recent news article:

    Earlier this year, the African country of Guinea-Bissau negotiated a deal with European and American waste brokers to accept a huge amount of waste from industrialized countries. The deal, *which reportedly would have brought the impoverished country payments greater than its gross national product*, was suspended after it was widely condemned by environmental groups. (emphasis added: 'Developing Countries Win Support for Curbs on Toxic Dumping', *New York Times*, 22 November 1988)

    Given the circumstances of this case, it is difficult to claim that the government of Guinea-Bissau would have been completely unreasonable had it finally accepted the offer.

19. See note 8.
20. Frank, p. 125, and Andrews, 'Ethics, Capitalism, and Multinationals' in Hoffmann, Lange and Fedo (1986) pp. 108–9.
21. Note, for example, M.K. Sheen's 'The Role of the Private Sector in Developing Countries: A World Bank Perspective' in Hoffmann, Lange and Fedo, (1986) pp. 231–8.
22. The difficulties faced by expatriate women in Saudi Arabia are vividly portrayed by Woodward (1980) pp. 162–75.
23. For a highly useful and illuminating discussion of these differences as found in the culture of Japan, see N. Hajime, 'Basic Features of Legal, Political, and Economic Thought of Japan' in Moore (1967) pp. 143–63. Also note Seward and Van Zandt (1985), especially pp. 53–67 and DeMente (1987) pp. 13–23.
24. Axtell (1985) pp. 111–19. Befu, however, offers a telling account of the difficulties this may cause: 'But because gift-giving is so pervasive in Japan, and the obligations to give, to receive, and to reciprocate are so strongly entrenched in the traditional social system, it is extremely difficult, if not impossible, to discern whether a gift is legitimate or illegitimate': 'Gift-Giving in a Modernizing Japan' in Lebra and Lebra (1974) pp. 209–21.
25. One corporate leader, Robert Grunts, has claimed success in coping with bribery by using the tactic of banding together with other corporations to resist: 'Ethics As A Way of Life' in Hoffmann, Lange and Fedo (1986) pp. 102–3.
26. However, Singapore has been cited as an example of a nation that has successfully eliminated corrupt practices through vigorous efforts: Frank (1980) p. 126.
27. 'Insider Trading, the Japanese Way', *New York Times* (10 August 1988).
28. In response to the Bhopal disaster, for instance, several corporations have announced that they will improve their standards of safety and strengthen their systems for monitoring compliance by their subsidiaries: 'An Industry Revamped By Disaster', *New York Times* (16 February 1989).

Chapter 5: Corporate Mobility

1. Donaldsen (1986) pp. 31–49; Flores (1986) pp. 50–9; 'Products Unsafe at Home Are Still Unloaded Abroad', *New York Times* (22 August 1982); and K.E. Goodpaster, 'Note on the Export of Pesticides from the United States to Developing Nations' in Hoffmann, Lange and Fedo (1986) pp. 305–33.
2. 'Many U.S. Companies Sell Products Abroad that are Barred Here', *The Wall Street Journal* (11 February 1971).
3. 'Bonn Will Tighten Curb on Exports of Deadly Goods', *New York Times* (11 January 1989) and 'U.S. Sees Gains in Effort to Stop West German Aid to Libya Chemical Plant', *New York Times* (14 January 1989).

Notes

4. 'F.D.A. Will Allow AIDS Patients to Import Unapproved Medicine', *New York Times* (24 July 1988); 'Tests of a Potential Drug for AIDS Beginning After Months of Delay', *New York Times* (24 July 1988); and 'U.S. Bans AIDS Drug from Canada', *New York Times* (2 August 1988).
5. J.E. Post, 'Ethical Dilemmas of Multinational Enterprises: An Analysis of Nestle's Traumatic Experiences With the Infant Formula Controversy', pp. 285–97 and C. Adelman, 'The Infant Formula Controversy: Everybody's Ethics', pp. 299–304, both in Hoffmann, Lange and Fedo (1986). See also S.P. Seth and J.E. Post, 'The Marketing of Infant Formula in Less Developed Countries' in Hoffmann and Moore (1976) pp. 427–37.
6. 'Europe's Failing Effort to Exile Toxic Trash', *New York Times* (16 October 1988). In one instance, hazardous waste *originated* in Italy, travelled to Nigeria, then circulated around Europe, and finally returned to a bemused Italy: 'Toxic Waste Boomerang: Ciao Italy!', *New York Times* (3 September 1988).
7. The UN Environment Program, for instance, is working toward completion of an international treaty to regulate the movement of hazardous waste across borders: 'Developing Countries Win Support for Curbs On Toxic Dumping', *New York Times* (22 November 1988).
8. Ibid.
9. Bertin and Wyatt (1988), and Walker and Bloomfield (1988).
10. 'Paris Conference Condemns the Use of Chemical Arms', *New York Times* (13 January 1989); 'U.N. Seeks Procedural Shifts for Poison Gas Investigations', *New York Times* (13 January 1989); J.G. Kester, 'Chemical Weapons, Cloudy Thinking', Op-Ed article in the *New York Times* (13 January 1989); and 'Chemical Arms: Third World Trend', *New York Times* (7 January 1989).
11. Ibid.
12. 'U.S. Again Reports Libyan Role in Terrorism', *New York Times* (19 January 1989).
13. For a broad ranging discussion of these matters, see H. Macdonald, 'The Strategic Goals of a Technology Embargo' in Schaffer (1985) pp. 208–40 and S.A. Merrill, 'The Internationalization of Technology' in Yochelson (1988) pp. 33–49.
14. The OECD has a standing Committee on Consumer Policy, which concerns itself with consumer safety among other matters. In 1979 the Secretary-General of the OECD noted that: 'The Council adopted a Recommendation [sic] to Member [sic] countries concerning, inter alia, the use of international safety standards, certification and prior approval of imported products and the prohibition of exports of dangerous goods which have been banned or withdrawn from sale in national markets': Report by the Secretary-General (1980) p. 33; see also UNCTC (1986) pp. 35–6.
15. OECD (1986) pp. 53–7 and UNCTC (1986) pp. 25–6.
16. The UN's Centre on Transnational Corporations has displayed considerable interest on these matters. Paragraphs 37–40 of the proposed UN Code of Conduct on Transnational Corporations are devoted to issues of consumer protection: UNCTC (1986) pp. 25–6.

17. 'Europe's Failing Effort to Exile Toxic Trash', *New York Times* (16 October 1988); Piasecki and Davis (1987) and Epstein, Brown and Pope (1982).
18. These difficulties receive attention in a number of works. One particularly thorough and comprehensive study is Wallace (1983).
19. The UN Department of Economic Affairs presently has an advisory service which was devised to assist nations negotiating agreements with multinational corporations: Feld (1980) pp. 122–3. Little would be required to expand this service to cover matters of taxation. The wealthy members of the OECD have formulated a model convention which establishes guidelines for tax arrangements: Vernon and Spar (1989) p. 122. However, the very poorest nations would require more elaborate institutional machinery to collect and transfer information, as well as provide assistance in matters of enforcement.
20. For an analysis of corporate decisions to seek labor outside their home nations, see M.T. Stanley, 'The Foreign Direct Investment Decision and Job Export as an Ethical Dilemma for the Multinational Corporation' in Hoffmann, Lange and Fedo (1986) pp. 493–509.

Chapter 6: Political Manipulation

1. As the final revisions were being made to this chapter, Noriega was removed from power by US armed forces. Prior to that, on 3 October 1989, Noriega ruthlessly crushed a coup attempt mounted by his own guards. Following that attempt, *The Economist* summarized the situation in Panama as follows:

    > The prospects for Panama are dim. American sanctions are failing to dislodge the general, though they are wearing down Panama's GDP (possibly by 10% this year). The IMF has cut Panama off because it is so deeply in arrears. An attempt by the Organization of American States to reach an agreement between the general and the opposition for new elections, superseding those which the opposition won on May 7th and the general annulled, flopped in August. Members of the opposition are too scared of being shot or beaten up to hold demonstrations. ('Still Snorting', *The Economist* 313, 7 October 1989, p. 52)

2. W.R. Doerner, 'Ignoring Both Carrot and Stick', *Time* 130 (5 October 1987) p. 36; P. Brimelow, 'Why South Africa Shrugs At Sanctions', *Forbes* 139 (9 March 1987) pp. 100–4; and 'How Do South African Sanctions Work?', *The Economist* 313 (14 October 1989) pp. 45–6. For a somewhat more positive view of the effect of the sanctions, however, see J. Kapstein, 'South Africa: The Squeeze Is On', *Business Week* (11 September 1989) pp. 44–5+.
3. Sampson (1975) pp. 260–7 and Tétreault (1975) p. 37.
4. Sampson (1975) pp. 269–82 and Emerson (1985).

5. D. Holloway, 'Western Technology and Soviet Military Power' in Schaffer (1985) pp. 170–87.
6. 'The Toshiba Scandal Has Exporters Running for Cover', *Business Week* (20 July 1987) pp. 86–7.
7. 'Iraq Said to Hold Advantage in War', *New York Times* (28 August 1984), and 'France Set to Press Iran on Hostages in Lebanon', *New York Times* (20 April 1986).
8. Ferrari, Knopf and Madrid (1987) pp. 157–74.
9. Relations between the United States and General Pinochet have been checkered. During the presidency of Jimmy Carter, relations reached a low ebb because of Pinochet's abysmal human rights record. With the ascendency of Ronald Reagan, relations immediately improved, though the administration eventually suggested that it might be a good thing if Pinochet relinquished power: Arriagada (1988) pp. 45–6.
10. 'Economic Collapse and Noriega Rule Producing Hopelessness in Panama', *New York Times* (16 January 1989) and 'Against the Odds, Panama's Economy Stays Afloat', *New York Times* (11 February 1989).
11. 'Bank Uncertainty in Panama', *New York Times* (10 August 1987).
12. Diskin and Sharpe (1986) and McClintock (1985).
13. J. Kapstein, 'South Africa: The Squeeze Is On', *op. cit.*, and 'Slash Ties, Apartheid Foes Urge', *New York Times* (2 February 1987).
14. Luban (1980) pp. 160–81; Beitz (1979) p. 79 n.; and Walzer (1977) pp. 98–9.
15. Walzer attributes this view to John Stuart Mill, and offers a useful analysis (1977) pp. 87–91.
16. The Sandinista movement was not supported by a number of ethnic groups living on the Atlantic coast of Nicaragua, for example. In fact, some offered armed resistance to it: J. Valenta and V. Valenta, 'The FSLN in Power', pp. 3–40 and M.C. Crahan, 'Political Legitimacy and Dissent', pp. 97–134, both in Valenta and Durán (1987) Freeland (1988).

    A significant number of colonists remained loyal to Great Britain during the American Revolution: 200000 served in the forces of rebellion, while 500000 remained loyal to Great Britain: Middlekauff (1982) p. 32, 547 and 549–50. Another scholar observes that some 19000 colonists served in various loyalist provincial corps: Calhoun (1973) p. 502.
17. See, for example, Milner (1989) pp. 46–72 and 186–212, and Huntford (1972).
18. Hudec (1975); Nau (1989); and OECD (1986).

Chapter 7: South Africa

1. GM, joined quickly by IBM, withdrew in late October of 1986. The exodus continued through the winter of 1987, though corporations continued to be chastised by critics for not totally severing their ties with South Africa: 'The Divestiture Con-Game', *New York Times* (16 December 1986) and 'Slash Ties, Apartheid Foes Urge', *New York Times* (2 February 1987).

2. There was no unanimity on this matter, of course. In an Op-Ed article in the *New York Times* Roger Smith, Chairman of GM, stated that GM's withdrawal was intended 'to send a signal that we are disappointed in the slow pace of progress [toward dismantling apartheid]': 'Why G.M. Decided to Quit South Africa' (30 October 1986). The chairman of IBM, however, avowed as emphatically that, 'We are not in business to conduct moral activity, we are not in business to conduct socially responsible action. We are in business to conduct business': *New York Times* (22 October 1986).
3. Fredrickson (1989) pp. 48–55.
4. The questions of the role of the black labor force in the South African economy and its importance for white prosperity has been carefully examined by Nattrass (1981); see also Seidman (1985) pp. 31–65.
5. Seidman (1985).
6. McCauley (1985) pp. 565–79.
7. Hare (1981) p. 7.
8. Report of the Study Commission on U.S. Policy Toward Southern Africa (1981) p. 80.
9. A listing of the Sullivan Principles, along with an account of their positive effects, is found in John Payton's 'Why United States Corporations Should Get Out of South Africa' in Hoffman and Moore (1976) pp. 401–6.
10. In response to GM's exit from South Africa, the director of the Interfaith Center on Corporate Responsibility noted, 'This is a tremendously significant decision. Business will understand the symbolism of the action, and we expect to see the trickle of companies leaving turn into a flood': 'G.M. Plans to Sell South Africa Unit to Local Group', *New York Times* (21 October 1986).
11. See, for example, Magorski (1974).
12. Thompson (1987), p. 20+.
13. An article by a director of the Americas Watch, for example, is entitled, 'No Pinochet, No Pinochetism', clearly making the linkage: *New York Times* (18 July 1987). See also Neier and Brown (1987) pp. 47–9.
14. 'Soviet Says U.N. Should Be Given Greater Powers', *New York Times* (8 October 1987).

Chapter 8: Conclusion

1. According to a report in the *New York Times*: 'Twenty-four nations plus the European Community signed the protocol today [16 Septemper 1987]. Forty-nine countries signed a document approving the meeting's actions, but some – including the Soviet Union – did not sign the protocol itself': 'Dozens of Nations Approve Accord to Protect Ozone' (17 Septemper 1987).
2. 'Mobil Reported to Plan South Africa Pullout', *New York Times* (27 April 1989), and 'Mobil Quitting South Africa, Blaming "Foolish" U.S. Laws', *New York Times* (29 April 1989).
3. See 'Part IV: Case Studies', pp. 249–73 in Hoffman, Moore and Fedo (1984).

References

Books

Arriagada, G., *Pinochet: The Politics of Power*, translated by N. Morris, V. Ercolando and K.A. Whitney (Boston: Unwin Hyman, 1988).
Axtell, R.E., *Do's and Taboos Around the World* (New York: John Wiley for the Parker Pen Company, 1985).
Barnet, R.J. and Müller, R.E., *Global Reach: The Power of The Multinational Corporations* (New York: Simon & Schuster, 1974).
Baum, W.C. and Tolbert, S.M., *Investing In Development* (Oxford: published for the World Bank by Oxford University, 1985).
Beauchamp, T.L. and Bowie, N.E. (eds) *Ethical Theory and Business* 2nd edn (Englewood Cliffs: Prentice-Hall, 1983).
Beitz, C., *Political Theory and International Relations* (Princeton: Princeton University, 1979).
Benewick, R. and Wingrove, P. (eds) *Reforming the Revolution* (London: Macmillan, 1988).
Bergsten, C.F., Horst, T. and Moran, T.H., *American Multinationals and American Interests* (Washington: The Brookings Institution, 1978).
Bertin, G.Y. and Wyatt, S., *Multinationals and Intellectual Property: The Control of the World's Technology* (Atlantic Highlands: Humanities, 1988).
Biberaj, E., *Albania Between East and West* (London: Institute for the Study of Conflict, 1986).
Boxi, U. and Paul T. (eds) *Mass Disasters and Multinational Liability: The Bhopal Case* (Bombay: N.M. Tripathi, 1986).
Bubnov, B., *Foreign Trade with the U.S.S.R.* (Oxford: Pergamon, 1987).
Calhoun, R.M., *The Loyalists in Revolutionary America, 1760–1781* (New York: Harcourt Brace Jovanovich, 1973).
Condon, J., *A Half Step Behind* (New York: Dodd Mead & Co., 1985).
Davids, J., *American Political and Economic Penetration of Mexico, 1877–1920* (New York: Arno 1976).
DeMente, B., *How to Do Business with the Japanese* (Lincolnwood: NTC Business Books, 1987).
DesJardins, J.R. and McCall, J.J. (eds) *Contemporary Issues in Business Ethics* (Belmont: Wadsworth, 1985).
Dessouki, A.E.H. (ed.) *Islamic Resurgence in the Arab World* (New York: Praeger, 1988).
Diskin, M. and Sharpe, K., *The Impact of U.S. Policy in El Salvador, 1979–1985* (Berkeley: Institute of International Studies, 1986).
Dworkin, R., *Taking Rights Seriously* (Cambridge: Harvard University, 1977).
Elfstrom, G., *Ethics for a Shrinking World* (London: Macmillan, 1990).
Emerson, S., *The American House of Saud* (New York: Franklin Watts, 1985).

Epstein, S.S., Brown, L.O. and Pope, C., *Hazardous Waste in America* (San Francisco: Sierra Club, 1982).
Esposito, J.L., *Islam and Politics*, revised 2nd edn (Syracuse: Syracuse University, 1987).
Feinberg, J., *Social Philosophy* (Englewood Cliffs: Prentice-Hall, 1973).
Feld, W.J., *Multinational Corporations and U.N. Politics* (New York: Pergamon Press, 1980).
Ferrari, P.L., Knopf, J.W. and Madrid, R.L., *U.S. Arms Exports: Policies and Contractors* (Washington: Investor Responsibility Research Center, 1987).
Foot, P., *Virtues and Vices* (Los Angeles: University of California, 1978)
Forbes, W.H., *Japan Today* (New York: Harper & Row, 1975).
Frank, I., *Foreign Enterprise in Developing Countries* (Baltimore and London: The Johns Hopkins University, 1980).
Freeland, J., *A Special Place in History* (London: Nicaragua Solidarity Campaign, 1988).
French, P.A., *Collective and Corporate Responsibility* (New York: Columbia University, 1984).
French, P.A., Uehling, T.E., Jr and Wettstein, H.K. (eds) *Ethical Theory: Character and Virtue*, Midwest Studies in Philosophy, XII (Notre Dame: University of Notre Dame, 1988).
Friedman, M., *Capitalism and Freedom* (Chicago: University of Chicago, 1962).
Gewirth, A., *Reason and Morality* (Chicago: University of Chicago, 1978).
Gillespie, N., 'Spindel Conference 1985: Moral Realism', *Southern Journal of Philosophy* XXIV, Supplement (1985).
Hare, R.M., *Moral Thinking* (Oxford: Oxford University, 1981).
Hertner, P. and Jones, G. (eds) *Multinationals: Theory and History* (Farnborough, Hants and Brookfield: Gower, 1986).
Hoffmann, W.M., Lange, A.E. and Fedo, D.A., *Ethics and the Multinational Enterprise* (Lanham, New York and London: University Press of America, 1986).
Hoffmann, W.M. and Moore, J.M., *Business Ethics* (New York: McGraw-Hill, 1976).
Hoffmann, W.M., Moore, J.M. and Fedo, D.A. (eds) *Corporate Governance and Institutionalizing Ethics* (Lexington: Lexington Books, 1984).
Hudec, R.E., *The GATT Legal System and World Trade Diplomacy* (New York, Washington and London: Praeger, 1975).
Humber, J. and Almeder, R. (eds) *Quantitative Risk Assessment: Biomedical Ethics Reviews, 1986* (Clifton: Humana, 1987).
Huntford, R., *The New Totalitarians* (New York: Stein & Day, 1972).
Joshi, B.R., *Untouchable!* (London: Zed Books, 1986).
Kant, I., *Foundations of the Metaphysics of Morals*, translation and introduction by L.W. Beck (Indianapolis: Bobbs-Merrill, 1959).
Knight, M.G., *How To Do Business With Russians* (Westport: Quorum Books, 1987).
Krasner, S.D., *Structural Conflict* (Berkeley, Los Angeles and London: University of California, 1985).
Law, S., *The New Multinationals: The Spread of Third World Enterprises* (New York: Wiley, 1983).

Lebra, J., Paulson, J. and Powers, E., *Women in Changing Japan* (Boulder: Westview, 1976).
Lebra, T.S. and Lebra, W.P. (eds) *Japanese Culture and Behavior* (Honolulu: University of Hawaii, 1974).
Lowrance, W.W., *Of Acceptable Risk* (Los Altos: William Kaufmann, 1976).
Luban, D., *Lawyers and Justice* (Princeton: Princeton University, 1988).
MacIntyre, A., *After Virtue* (Notre Dame: University of Notre Dame, 1981).
Magorski, Z., *The Psychology of East–West Trade* (New York: Mason & Lipscomb, 1974).
Mahar, J.M., *The Untouchables in Contemporary India* (Tucson: University of Arizona, 1972).
McClintock, M., *The American Connection: Vol. I: State Terror and Popular Resistance in El Salvador* (London: Zed Books, 1985).
Mernissi, F., *Beyond the Veil*, revised edn (Bloomington and Indianapolis: Indiana University, 1987).
Middlekauff, R., *The Glorious Cause* (New York and Oxford: Oxford University, 1982).
Milner, H., *Sweden: Social Democracy in Practice* (Oxford: Oxford University, 1989).
Minai, N., *Women in Islam* (New York: Seaview Books, 1981).
Mitchell, R.H., *The Korean Minority in Japan* (Berkeley and Los Angeles: University of California, 1967).
Moore, C.A. (ed.) *The Mind of Japan* (Honolulu: University of Hawaii, 1967).
Moore, G.E., *Principia Ethica* (Cambridge: Cambridge University, 1903).
Myers, R.J. (ed.) *The Political Morality of the International Monetary Fund* (New Brunswick and Oxford: Transaction Books, 1987).
Nader, R., Petkas, P.J. and Blackwell, K. (eds) *Whistleblowing: The Report of the Conference on Professional Responsibility* (New York: Grossman, 1972).
Nattrass, J., *The South African Economy* (Cape Town: Oxford University, 1981).
Nau, H.R., *Domestic Trade Politics and The Uruguay Round* (New York: Columbia University, 1989).
OECD, *The OECD Guidelines for Multinational Enterprises* (Paris: OECD, 1986).
OECD, *The OECD Guidelines for Multinational Enterprises* (Paris: OECD, 1986).
Peters, C. and Branch, T., *Blowing the Whistle: Dissent in the Public Interest* (New York: Praeger, 1972).
Piasecki, B.W. and Davis, G.A. (eds) *America's Future in Toxic Waste Management: Lessons From Europe* (New York: Quorum Books, 1987).
Rahman, A. (ed.) *Role of Muslim Women in Society* (London: Seerah Foundation, 1986).
Rawls, J., *A Theory of Justice* (Cambridge: Harvard University, 1971).
Regan, T. (ed.) *Just Business* (Philadelphia: Temple University, 1983).
Reischauer, E.O., *Japan: The Story of a Nation*, revised edn (New York: Knopf, 1974).
Reischauer, E.O., *The Japanese Today* (Cambridge and London: Harvard University, 1988).

Report by the Secretary-General, *Activities of the OECD in 1979* (Paris: OECD, 1980).
Report of the Study Commission on U.S. Policy Toward Southern Africa, *South Africa: Time Running Out* (Berkeley and Los Angeles: University of California, 1981).
Richards, D.A.J., *A Theory of Reasons for Action* (Oxford: Oxford University, 1971).
Rodinson, M., *Islam and Capitalism*, translated by B. Pearce (Austin: University of Texas, 1978).
Sampson, A., *The Seven Sisters* (New York: Viking, 1975).
Sampson, A., *The Sovereign State of I.T.T.* (London: Hodder & Stoughton, 1973).
Sayre-McCord, G., *Essays on Moral Realism* (Ithaca: Cornell University, 1988).
Schaffer, M.E. (ed.) *Technology Transfer and East-West Relations* (New York: St. Martin's Press, 1985).
Schrader-Frechette, K.S, *Risk Analysis and Scientific Method* (Hingham: D. Reidel, 1985).
Seidman, A., *The Roots of Crisis in Southern Africa* (Trenton: Africa World Press, 1985).
Seward, J. and Van Zandt, H., *Japan: The Hungry Guest* (Tokyo: Lotus, 1985).
Shue, H., *Basic Rights* (Princeton: Princeton University, 1980).
Sidell, S.R., *The IMF and Third-World Political Instability* (London: Macmillan, 1988).
Sigmund, P.E., *Multinationals in Latin America* (Madison: University of Wisconsin, 1980).
Simon, J.G., Powers, C. and Gunneman, J.P., *The Ethical Investor* (New Haven: Yale University, 1972).
Sobel, R., *I.T.T.* (New York: Truman Nalley–Times Books, 1982).
Stavis, B., *China's Political Reforms* (New York, Westport and London: Praeger, 1988).
Steinberg, D. I., *Burma's Road Toward Development* (Boulder: Westview, 1981).
Tétreault, M.A., *Revolution in the World Petroleum Market* (Westport and London: Quorum Books, 1975).
United Nations Commission for Latin America, *Five Studies on the Situation of Women in Latin America* (New York: United Nations, 1983).
UNCTC, *Foreign Direct Investment, the Service Sector and International Banking* (New York: United Nations, May 1987).
UNCTC, *Transnational Corporations in World Development, Third Survey* (New York: United Nations, 1983).
UNCTC, *The United Nations Code of Conduct on Transnational Corporations* (New York: United Nations, 1986).
Valenta, J. and Durán, E. (eds) *Conflict in Nicaragua* (Boston: Allen & Unwin, 1987).
Vernon, R., *Sovereignty at Bay: The Multinational Spread of U.S. Enterprises* (New York: Basic Books, 1971).
Vernon, R., *Storm Over the Multinationals* (Cambridge: Harvard University, 1977).

Vernon, R. and Spar, D.L., *Beyond Globalism: Remaking American Foreign Policy* (New York: The Free Press, 1989).
Walker, C.E. and Bloomfield, M.A., *Intellectual Property Rights and Capital Formation in the Next Decade* (Lanham, New York and London: University Press of America, 1988).
Wallace, C.D., *Legal Control of the Multinational Enterprise* (The Hague: Martinus Nijhoff, 1983).
Walzer, M., *Just and Unjust Wars* (New York: Basic Books, 1977).
Westshore, Inc. (ed.) *Doing Business With the Russians* (New York: Praeger, 1978).
Wilson, R., *Islamic Business: Theory and Practice*, revised edn (London: The Economist Intelligence Unit, 1985).
Woodward, P.N., *Oil and Labor in the Middle East* (New York: Praeger, 1980).
Yochelson, J. (ed.) *Keeping Pace* (Cambridge: Ballinger, 1988).

Articles

Ajami, F., 'Iran: The Impossible Revolution', *Foreign Affairs* 67 (Winter 1988/89) pp. 135–55.
Arnesen, A., 'Perspective of Norwegian Development Aid in the 1980s', in J.R. Parkensen (ed.) *Poverty and Aid* (Oxford: Basil Blackwell, 1983).
Burton, R.G., 'Neointuitionism: The Neglected Moral Realism', *Southern Journal of Philosophy* 25 (Summer 1987) pp. 147–52.
Donaldsen, T., 'The Ethics of Risk in the Global Economy', *Business & Professional Ethics Journal* 5 (1986) pp. 31–49.
Elliston, F.A., 'Anonymous Whistleblowing: A Conceptual and Ethical Analysis', *Business and Professional Ethics Journal* 1 (Winter 1982) pp. 39–58.
Elliston, F.A., 'Anonymy and Whistleblowing', *Journal of Business Ethics* 1 (August 1982) pp. 67–177.
Flores, A., 'Commenting on Donaldsen: Ethics and the Exportation of Banned Pesticides', *Business & Professional Ethics Journal* 5 (1986) pp. 50–9.
Frederickson, G.M., 'Can South Africa Change?', *New York Review of Books* 36 (26 October 1989) pp. 48–55.
Friedman, M., 'The Social Responsibility of Business Is to Increase Its Profits', *New York Times Magazine* (13 September 1970) pp. 32–3 and 122 ff.
Goodwin, R.N., 'Letter From Peru', *New Yorker* 45 (17 May 1969) pp. 41–6+.
Heenan, D.A. and Keegan, W.J., 'The Rise of Third World Multinationals', in P.A. Grub, F. Ghadar and D. Khambata (eds) *The Multinational Enterprise in Transition*, 3rd edn (Princeton: Darwin, 1986) pp. 497–312.
Levitt, T., 'The Dangers of Social Responsibility', *Harvard Business Review* (September–October, 1958).
Leys, S., 'The Curse of the Man Who Could See the Little Fish at the Bottom of the Ocean', *New York Review of Books* 36 (20 July 1989) p. 29.
Luban, D., 'Just War and Human Rights', *Philosophy & Public Affairs* 9 (Winter 1980) pp. 160–81.
MacFarquhar, R., 'The End of the Chinese Revolution', *New York Review of Books* 36 (20 July 1989) pp. 8–10.

McCauley, R.N., 'The Moral Status of Apartheid: Can the Presence of Foreign Corporations in South Africa Be Morally Justified?', *Canadian Journal of Philosophy* 15 (December 1985) pp. 565–79.

Neier, A. and Brown, C., 'Pinochet's Way', *New York Review of Books* 34 (25 June 1987) pp. 47–9.

Reddaway, P., 'The Threat to Gorbachev', *New York Review of Books* 36 (17 August 1989) pp. 19–24.

Sakharov, A., 'A Speech to the People's Congress', translated by E. Kline, *New York Review of Books* 36 (17 August 1989) pp. 25–6.

Schell, O., 'Letters From the Other China', *New York Review of Books* 36 (20 July 1989) pp. 32–3.

Spero, J.E., 'Guiding Global Finance', *Foreign Policy* 73 (Winter 1988/89) pp. 114–34.

Thompson, L., 'Before the Revolution', *New York Review of Books* 34 (11 July 1987) p. 20+.

Index

affirmative action, 33, 49
 see also discrimination
African National Congress, 90
agreements, contractual, 86–7, 88–9
AIDS, 64
Albania, 1
Allende, Salvador, 31–2
apartheid, 50, 55, 79, 90–9, 104, 118, 132
 and corporations, 90, 92–3, 95–6
 moral wrong of, 91–2, 97
 role of corporations in preserving, 93, 94, 96–7
 see also discrimination; South Africa
Arabia, 77–8
Arab oil embargo of 1973, 3, 77–8, 127
Argentina, 42, 123
autonomy, 2, 8, 25, 84–6, 107

Bangladesh, 52
Bentham, Jeremy, 91
Bhopal, 37, 38, 45, 46, 103, 105, 122–3, 128
Bhutto, Benazir, 49
Boisjoly, Roger, 118
Brazil, 50, 56
bribery, 50–1, 54, 55, 58–61, 100, 117–18, 127, 128
 distinguished from gift-giving, 59, 127
 and governments, 60
 harm of, 59–60
 moral wrong of, 58
 and multinational corporations, 50–1, 58–9, 117–18
Burakumin, 125
 see also Eta; Japan
Bush, President George, 98

Cambodia, 96

Canada
 as home nation, 10
 as host nation, 3, 10, 112
Chile, 31–2, 81–2, 96
China, 38, 59, 95, 96, 112, 126
commerce, multinational, 2, 4–7, 13, 71, 73–6, 87, 97, 106–7, 112, 121
 conditions of, 2–3, 4–7, 10, 12–13, 23, 24, 25, 26, 27, 35–6, 41–2, 45, 47, 68–9, 71, 100, 102, 104–6, 111–12
 ethics of, 2–3, 7, 9–10, 26, 100, 101
 evolution of, 4–7, 8–9, 71, 74–6, 100, 115–6
 legal regulation of, 106
corporations, 12
 actions of, 14–15, 20
 and apartheid, 90, 92–3, 95–6
 as artificial persons, 17
 benefits for South Africa of, 92–3, 94
 benefits to from activity in South Africa, 92–3
 compared with governments, 17, 33
 compared with individual persons, 13–14, 17, 25, 72
 compared with military forces, 33
 and competition, 12, 16–18, 23, 35, 73–4, 102, 114, 116, 121
 cooperation among, 18, 35, 59, 69, 73, 114, 117, 118, 121, 128
 culture of, 25, 117, 118, 120
 death of, 16, 17–18, 117
 developing moral sensitivity of, 7–8, 12, 15–6, 19–23, 118, 119
 moral agency of, 12, 13–16, 33–4, 67, 116, 117

139

corporations *cont.*
  obligation to avoid harm of, 32, 33–4, 43, 67
  obligations of, 30–4, 62, 67–8, 69, 70, 75–6, 88–9, 98, 117
  and persons within them, 13–15, 19–22, 30–4, 67, 68–9, 88–9, 107, 117, 118
  and profits, 12, 16, 18–19, 23
  self-interest of, 75
  self-preservation of, 16–18
  right to existence of, 17
  role of in preserving apartheid, 93, 94, 96–7
  special responsibilities of, 19
corporations, multinational, 1–2, 3–4, 8–9, 12, 48, 100, 108, 112, 113–14, 115–16, 120, 121–2, 123, 124, 126, 127, 131, 132
  benefits from, 7, 38–40, 55, 95, 112
  and bribery, 50–1, 58–9, 117–18
  codes of conduct for, 7, 9, 57–8, 60, 68, 101, 105, 114–15, 117, 129
  compared with domestic corporations, 23, 40, 73, 123
  definition of, 111–12
  and developing nations, 7, 63, 123, 124
  and development, economic, 3, 38–9, 40–1, 42, 43–4, 64–5, 114
  enforcement of obligations, 68, 107
  and governments, 3, 5, 36–8, 40, 41, 48, 55, 67–8, 75, 77–8, 79–80, 81–3, 84, 86–7, 100–1, 104, 113, 115–16, 120, 122, 123, 127, 130
  harm caused by, 1–2, 5, 13, 36, 71–2, 75–6, 77, 108–9, 112
  harm to advanced nations from, 3, 6, 36, 63, 64, 66, 71, 74, 116–17
  harm to poor nations from, 3, 36–8, 43, 63, 64, 65, 66, 71, 74, 122–3, 123–4
  and home governments, 41, 55, 60–1, 120
  and imperialism, 3, 6, 114, 115
  influence of, 36–7, 121–2
  and labor, 5, 61, 73–6
  and law, 48, 71, 122, 128
  legal control of, 5, 36, 37–8, 45–7, 63, 71–3, 75, 101, 106, 122–3, 125
  and militant nationalism, 6, 41
  moral responsibility of, 12–33, 60–1, 62, 69–70, 72, 75–6, 90, 97, 98, 117, 118
  moral standards of, 48, 50, 56–7, 60–1, 101–4, 117, 118
  obligations of, 4, 43, 47, 48, 54–5, 60–1, 62, 80, 88–9, 94–5
  and persons within them, 12–13, 68–9, 80, 88–9, 107, 118
  and profits, 6, 12, 52, 62, 71–2
  size of, 35–8, 113, 121
  taxation of, 5, 71–3, 130
  and weapons sales policy, 79–80, 89, 116–17
culture, 48–51, 57
  business, 58–9, 60, 128
  of corporations, 25, 117, 118, 120
  Islamic, 49, 126–7
  moral, 60
cyclamates, 63
  see also products, hazardous

debt crisis, international, 42, 44–5, 123
de Klerk, F.W., 95
development, economic, 3, 6, 7, 38–9, 41–5, 54, 74, 100, 113, 114, 124–5
  definition of, 39
  and governments, 43
  and multinational corporations, 3, 38–9, 40–1, 42, 43–4, 64–5, 114
  strategies for, 42–3
discrimination, 33, 55, 56–8
  racial, 49–50, 56, 86, 90–9
  sexual, 49–50, 56, 125
  see also affirmative action; apartheid; South Africa
distributive justice, 51, 61

duty to preserve human life, 19,
    28–30, 52, 54, 61, 62, 67, 75, 80,
    87–8
  characteristics of, 28–9
  as fundamental, 28, 30, 53, 62, 67,
    75
  see also obligations; wants, basic
Dworkin, Ronald, 26

economy, single world–wide, 1, 3, 7,
    35, 63, 101, 104–6, 111, 112,
    113
  evolution of, 1, 3, 7, 8–9, 35, 45,
    71, 74–5, 104–6, 107, 112,
    115–16, 121
Egypt, 49
El Salvador, 83
embargo, economic, 77, 79, 81–3, 87
  harm of for Panama, 82–3, 130
  see also sanctions, economic
equality, sexual, 49
Eta, 125
  see also *Burakumin*; Japan
Europe, 1, 3, 5, 8, 41, 49, 50, 51,
    52–3, 58, 64, 77, 79, 126, 129,
    132
  and multinational commerce, 5,
    121, 126
  and sexual equality, 49

Feinberg, Joel, 26
Ford, Henry, 15
France, 79, 124–5
Friedman, Milton, 34

General Agreement on Tariffs and
    Trade (GATT), 9, 42, 87, 106
General Motors (GM), 18, 20, 114,
    117, 131, 132
Germany, 61, 64, 109, 112
gift-giving, 58–9, 127
  see also bribery; culture, business
Gorbachev, Mikhail, 1, 98, 126, 127
governments, national, 17, 33, 39,
    42, 43–4, 59–60, 81, 83–9, 100,
    108, 118, 123
  altering the conduct of, 86
  and bribery, 60
  and development, economic, 43

distinguished from citizens, 17,
    53–4, 71–3, 84–6, 108–9
  external influences on, 44–5, 84,
    86–9
  legitimacy of, 84–6, 94, 126
  and multinational corporations,
    3–4, 5, 9, 36–8, 40, 47, 48, 55,
    60–1, 67–8, 69, 71–3, 75–6,
    77–8, 79–80, 81–3, 84, 86–9,
    100–1, 104, 105, 106, 115–16,
    120, 122, 123, 126, 127, 130
  and regulation of weapons
    transfer, 66–7, 79–81
  responsibility of, 59–60, 69, 70,
    75–6, 87, 97, 98, 105, 120,
    124–5
  role of, 45, 83–9
  sovereignty of, 5, 43–4, 80–1,
    84–86, 101
  and taxes, 71–2
Great Britain, 52, 65, 123, 131
  as home nation, 10, 112
  as host nation, 10
Group of Seven, 44, 124–5
Guinea-Bissau, 65, 127

Hare, R.M., 27, 91
Harijan, 125
  see also Untouchables; India
Helms, Senator Jesse, as admirer of
    dictator, 82
heroism, moral, 20–1, 102
Hobbes, Thomas, 16, 17
Hobbesian situation, 16–18
home nations, 3, 5, 6–7, 9, 10, 31,
    36, 40, 41, 77, 89, 112, 113, 114
host nations, 3, 5, 6–7, 9, 10, 36–8,
    40, 41, 42–3, 52, 57, 58, 59, 72,
    77, 78, 112, 113, 114
human nature
  basic requirements of, 25, 28–9,
    52–3, 55
  limitations of, 2, 28–9, 109–10

ideology, 4, 27, 50–1, 60–1, 95
India, 37, 45–6, 49, 112, 122–3, 125
  as home nation, 10
  as host nation, 10
  legal system of, 37, 45–6, 122–3

intellectual property, 66
International Business Machines (IBM), 131, 132
International Labor Organization (ILO), 108
International Monetary Fund (IMF), 9, 42, 44, 124, 130
International Telephone & Telegraph (ITT), 31–2
intuitionism, 24–5, 119
  defined, 24
  limitations of, 24
  role of within mature moral order, 31
Iran, 39, 50, 79
Iraq, 79, 96
Islam, 50, 51, 57, 79, 84, 95, 126–7
Israel, 77, 127
Italy, 65, 129

Japan, 5, 49, 59–60, 78, 109, 112, 116–17, 124, 125, 128

Kant, Immanuel, 8, 25, 107, 119
Korea, South, 49, 95
  as home nation, 10
  as host nation, 10

labor, 5, 40, 51–2, 75–6, 91, 132
  costs of, 73–4
  and multinational corporations, 5, 61, 73–6
  safety rules for, 51–2, 53–4, 61–2, 100
  unions of, 53
  wages of, 51–2, 53, 61–2, 73, 92
Latin America, 41, 49, 79, 81, 82, 83, 121–2
  and multinational corporations, 41, 115–16, 121–2
law, international, 46–7
Lebanon, 79
Libya, 66, 79, 126–7

managers, corporate, 15, 18, 22, 33, 104, 117
  duty to seek profits of, 18–19, 23, 52
  responsibilities of, 12, 18–19, 52, 67, 117
Marcos, Ferdinand, 96
Marxism, 1, 50–1, 84
medicines, 64–5, 69
Menem, Carlos Saúl, 123
Mexico, 50, 55, 117–18
Middle East, 31, 59, 77–8, 79
Mill, John Stuart, 131
Mitterrand, François, 124–5
Mobil Oil, 104
moral agency, 12–16, 54, 56, 102–3
  corporate, 12, 13–16, 17, 19, 22–3, 33–4, 67
  corporate compared with personal, 13–15, 17, 22–3
  and obligation to feel shame, 93–4
morally obtuse, the, 103–4
  and multinational commerce, 103
moral order, mature, 7–10, 13, 22–3, 24, 25, 58, 60, 97, 99, 102–4, 106–10
  compared with moral anarchy, 8
  contrasted with ideal moral condition, 8
  costs of absence, 68–9, 103
  criticism of, 8, 108–9
  defining features of, 7–8, 108
  hazards to development of, 106
  of institutions, compared with persons, 107
  and Kant's kingdom of ends, 8
  means of enforcement within, 107
  and multinational commerce, 24, 57–8, 97, 107–10
  role of intuitions within, 24
  and specific moral practises, 9
moral standards, 15, 48, 56–7, 105, 108
  cost of for corporations, 50, 69, 117
  disagreement concerning, 69, 104, 107
  enforcement of, 101, 107
  of multinational corporations, 48, 50, 56–7, 60–1, 101–4, 117, 118
  strategies for developing, 69, 107, 118, 119

moral uncertainty, 102
Morton Thiokol, 21, 118

national security, 64, 66, 67, 69, 78, 79, 81, 85, 113
Nationalist Party, 90, 91
Nestlé Infant Formula, 65
Nicaragua, 84, 131
Nigeria, 129
Noriega, General Manuel, 3, 130
  and the United States, 77, 81–3, 89

obligations, 52
  of corporations, 30–4, 62, 67–8, 69, 70, 75–6, 88–9, 98, 117
  enforcement of, 68
  fundamental, 30–1, 52, 87
  moral justification of, 130
  of multinational corporations, 4, 43, 47, 48, 54–5, 60–1, 62, 80, 88–9, 94–5
  special, 19, 30–1, 34, 61, 67, 87–8
  weight of, 19, 30–1, 34, 67, 87–8
  see also duty, to preserve human life; wants, basic
Organization for Economic Development and Cooperation (OECD), 69, 87, 114, 115, 129, 130
  Committee on Consumer Policies of, 68, 129

Pakistan, 49
Pan-Africanist Movement, 90
Panama, 3, 130
  and the United States, 77, 81–3, 87, 89
Panama Canal, 81, 82
Persian Gulf War, 79
pesticides, 63, 65
Philippines, 50, 55, 96
Pinochet, General Augusto, 81–2, 96, 131
pollution, environmental, 2, 33, 53, 61–2, 100, 101, 103
Pol Pot, 96

products
  enforcement of standards for, 64–5, 70
  hazardous, 2, 63, 64, 65, 67–8, 129
  safety of, international standards for, 64–5, 67–8, 69, 70, 129

revolution, 85–6
  American, 84, 131
rights, theories of, 24, 25–6, 120
  limitations of, 25–6
  manifesto sense of, 26
risk, appropriate level of, 53–4, 61–2, 65–6, 68–9, 127

sanctions, economic, 3, 77, 81–3, 130
  see also embargo, economic
Sandinistas, 84, 88, 131
Saudi Arabia, 49, 57, 126–7, 128
shame, 93–4
Sha'ria, 51, 126–7
  see also Islam
Singapore, 128
South Africa, 3, 7, 20, 21, 50, 56–7, 77, 79, 83, 89, 90–9, 103, 104, 131, 132
  benefits of corporate activity for, 92–3, 94
  benefits to corporations from activity in, 92–3
  distinctive character of, 95–6
  lessons of for future moral sensibility, 98–9
  see also apartheid; discrimination; symbolism
sovereignty, 5, 43–4, 80–1, 82, 84–5
  advantages of for governments, 72–3, 84–6, 107
  see also governments, national
Soviet Union, 38, 67, 78–9, 95, 96, 98, 109, 112, 116–17, 126, 127, 132
standard of human life
  minimal, 39, 52–3, 55, 61
state of nature, Hobbesian, 16–17
stockholders, 15, 17, 19, 21–2, 103–4
  and South Africa, 22, 104, 118

Sullivan Principles, 92, 93, 132
Sweden, 85
symbolism, 93, 97, 99
 and South Africa, 93, 96, 98, 99, 132
Syria, 96

taxes, 5, 130
 and governments, 71–2
 just rates of, 71–2, 73
 and multinational corporations, 5, 71–3, 130
technology, 66, 67, 78, 81, 106, 111
Tiananmen Square, 95, 126
toleration, 56, 57
Toshiba Machine, 116–17
Toyota, 18, 114, 117

Union Carbide, 37, 122–3
 see also Bhopal; India
United Nations, 9, 44, 45–6, 98, 101, 108, 111, 114–15, 125, 129, 130
 Centre for Transnational Corporations of, 69, 129
 Code of Conduct on Transnational Corporations of, 68, 114–15, 121, 123, 129
 and issues of multinational commerce, 9, 104
 role in standards of product safety, 70
 Universal Declaration of Human Rights of, 26, 61
United States, 8, 22, 37, 52, 63, 64, 67, 90, 98, 109, 112–13, 118, 121, 122, 131
 and control of technology transfer, 67, 78–9, 116–17
 as home nation, 3, 10, 77–8, 112–13
 as host nation, 3, 10, 112–13
 and Latin America, 41, 115–16
 and Panama, 3, 77, 81–3, 87, 89, 130
 role in multinational commerce, 4–5, 113, 115–16
 and sexual equality, 49
 symbolic tie to apartheid, 93
 and Watergate, 22, 97
 and weapons transfer, 78, 79
Untouchables, 125
 see also Harijan; India
USSR, see Soviet Union
utilitarianism, 24, 25, 26–30, 91–2
 and apartheid, 91–2
 limitations of, 27
 and preferences, 27–30, 91
 and rights, 25
 see also wants

virtue-based ethics, 24–5, 119
 limitations of, 24–5, 119

wants
 basic, 28–31
 basic compared with secondary, 29–30, 54
 obligation to supply secondary, 29–30, 34, 54
 secondary, 29–30
 see also duty to preserve human life; obligations; utilitarianism
wastes, hazardous, 63, 65–6, 70, 101, 109, 127, 129
 standards for management of, 65–6, 70–1, 129
Watergate, 22, 97
 see also United States
weapons
 atomic, 79
 chemical, 66–7, 79
 trade in, 2, 78–81, 103, 109
whistle-blowers, 20–1, 118
whistle-blowing, 20, 31
 defined, 118
workers, see labor
World Bank, 9, 42, 44, 124, 125

Zia, General Mohammad, 49